Hamlyn
HISTORY OF TRAINS

Hamlyn
HISTORY
OF TRAINS

Colin Garratt

HAMLYN

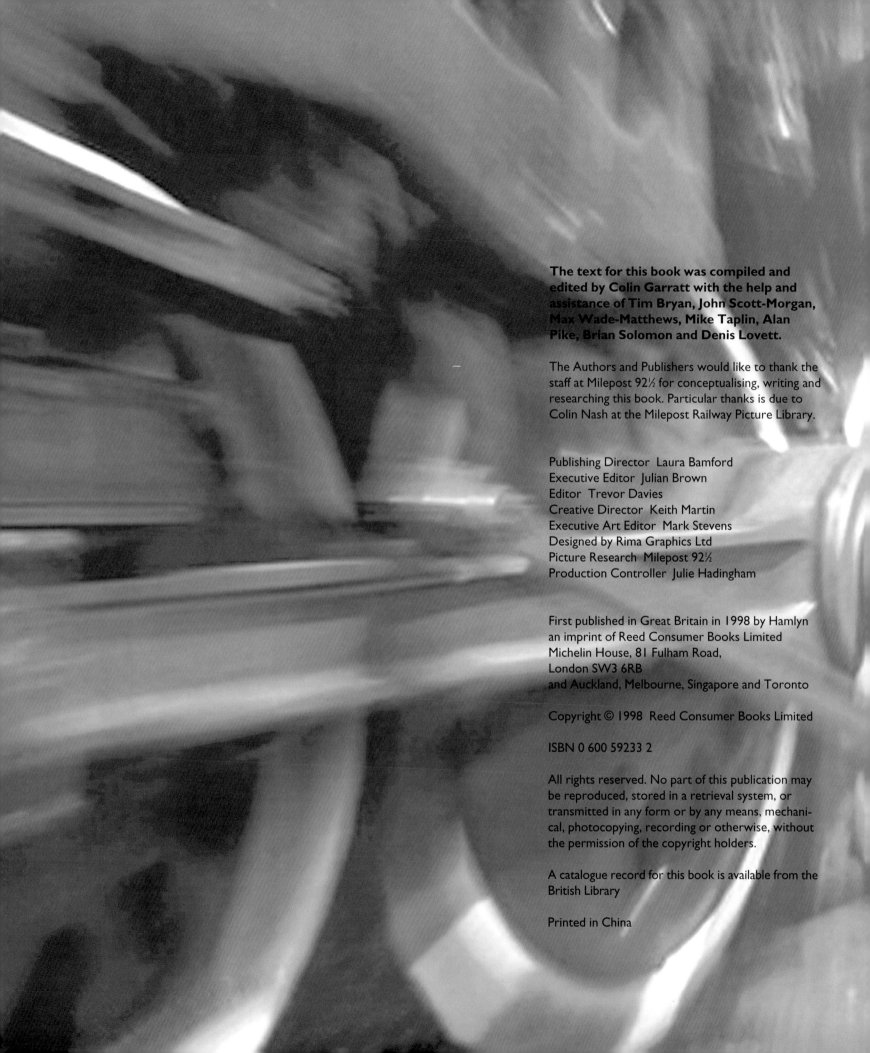

The text for this book was compiled and edited by Colin Garratt with the help and assistance of Tim Bryan, John Scott-Morgan, Max Wade-Matthews, Mike Taplin, Alan Pike, Brian Solomon and Denis Lovett.

The Authors and Publishers would like to thank the staff at Milepost 92½ for conceptualising, writing and researching this book. Particular thanks is due to Colin Nash at the Milepost Railway Picture Library.

Publishing Director Laura Bamford
Executive Editor Julian Brown
Editor Trevor Davies
Creative Director Keith Martin
Executive Art Editor Mark Stevens
Designed by Rima Graphics Ltd
Picture Research Milepost 92½
Production Controller Julie Hadingham

First published in Great Britain in 1998 by Hamlyn an imprint of Reed Consumer Books Limited
Michelin House, 81 Fulham Road,
London SW3 6RB
and Auckland, Melbourne, Singapore and Toronto

CONTENTS

1 Evolution of the LOCOMOTIVE

THE OPENING OF THE WORLD'S FIRST public steam line, the Stockton & Darlington Railway, on 27 September 1825, is seen by most historians as the beginning of the Age of Railways. The run by George Stephenson's *Locomotion No. 1* on that notable day was, however, only one step in a journey that had begun many years before. Although it is thought that wheeled trucks and wooden tracks were in use in mines in Germany as early as the 12th century, it was not until the 17th century that they became common in the coal mining areas of North East England. In the 18th century the wooden rails were replaced by cast iron which made them more durable and stronger, leaving the way open for the locomotives which were to come in the early 19th century.

Early Locomotives

The first steam locomotive to run on rails was that designed by Richard Trevithick, a Cornish engineer, in 1804 for the South Wales Pen-y-Darren Iron Works. However, the weight of the locomotive, adapted from a stationary steam engine, shattered the tracks, effectively delaying the birth of rail travel for another two decades.

The first successful locomotives were built in the North East of England. Colliery engines, such as John Blenkinsop's locomotives of 1811, and William Hedley's *Puffing Billy* and *Wylam Dilly* of 1813, inspired George Stephenson, a young colliery engineer from Northumberland, to design and build his own steam locomotives, a new career that was to make Stephenson world famous and to this day he is recognised as the 'Father of the Railways'.

In spite of the success of *Locomotion No. 1* the Stockton & Darlington Railway did not become the world's first steam-worked 'intercity' passenger line, for after the inaugural run passenger services reverted to horse power. It was not until the opening of the Liverpool & Manchester Railway, in September 1830, that what we would call a modern main line passenger railway came into existence. Designed by Stephenson, the Liverpool & Manchester overcame considerable engineering difficulties, including that of traversing Chat Moss Bog, and utilised new and more reliable steam locomotives, such as the *Rocket*, which was designed by George Stephenson's son, Robert.

France

In the rest of Europe, the introduction of steam railways did not lag far behind Great Britain. The first railway in France, running from St Etienne to Andriezieux, officially opened, using horse power, in October 1828. In comparison with other countries, progress in France was slow, as by 1850, there were still only 1,927 miles of railway in that country, as compared with over 6,600 in Britain. British interests continued to influence the development of railways in France, with civil and locomotive engineers, finance and even British navvies being used to construct new lines.

The United States

Once they had been established in England, it was not long before railways spread to the other side of the Atlantic. The first railroad to open in the United States was the Baltimore & Ohio, which began operation, using horses, in April 1827. The first locomotives, however, did not arrive until 1829 and the honour of being the first steam locomotive to run on a railway in the United States fell to the *Stourbridge Lion*, one of four purchased from England for use on the Delaware & Hudson Railroad. Ironically the engine proved to be too heavy for the rails, which were constructed of wood with iron strips, and the railway had to revert to horse-power for several more years.

The Baltimore & Ohio Railroad was the location for the inaugural public run, on 25 August 1830, of the first American-built locomotive – Peter Cooper's *Tom Thumb*. Within a year, railways in the US were becoming firmly established when two further companies, the Camden & Amboy and the Mohawk & Hudson, introduced steam traction.

Below: **Before the power of steam was used for traction, it had been employed for many years to work stationary engines, particularly in collieries. Here we see one such at a pit head with winding gear c.1820.**

RAILWAY MANIA

Above: By the mid-1930s, Stephenson had produced a 2–2–2 passenger locomotive which became an established design in Britain and a well-known export type. An example was *Der Adler*, that was exported to Germany and used for the opening of the first German Railway line, between Nuremberg and Fürth, in 1835. The foreground shows State President, von Stichauer, talking to Johannes Scharrer, the railway's architect.

Left: George Hudson (1800–1871) was a shopkeeper who, after receiving a legacy, became a railway share speculator. It was not long before, by dint of forcing down rival companies' shares, and then buying them up, he controlled 20% of England's railways. A Member of Parliament, his business came to an inglorious end when it was discovered that he had been paying dividends out of capital and enriching himself at his shareholders' expense.

THE CAUTION AND SUSPICION with which railways had been viewed initially soon disappeared. Not only were the general public accepting railways, but by the early 1840s, investors were also realising that there was money to be made from them. What followed was a massive speculative boom, fuelled by a feeling, encouraged by the press, that railways were one of the safest and securest inventions in existence and an emblem of 'peace and prosperity'.

George Hudson – the Railway King

With feelings running so high, a plethora of railway schemes were put forward, many with little or no chance of ever succeeding. In 1845 *The Times* reported that over 600 new lines were already proposed, with another 600 likely to be adopted. What became known as 'Railway Mania' spread through Britain, and many people speculated their life's savings. The mania was short lived and when the Bank of England raised its interest rate in 1847 panic set in and the less prudent lost all they had. Some, like George Hudson, a businessman from York, made considerable sums from investing in new schemes, so much so that by 1846 it was estimated that he controlled nearly half of England's railways. Many of the methods used by the 'Railway King', as he became known, were less than honest and his fall from grace, when it came, mirrored that of the railway mania itself.

Europe

Away from France, railways in Europe grew at an alarming rate. In Germany, great excitement surrounded the construction of the first steam railway in Bavaria, which ran from Nuremberg to Furth. Although rolling stock and rails were made in Germany, the locomotive used to haul the first train on 7 December 1835, was a Robert Stephenson & Company's 'Patentee' design named *Der Adler*. The railway, named the 'Ludwigsbahn' in

honour of the King of Bavaria, also took the opportunity to hire a British driver, a Mr Wilson, who, impressed by both the wages and prestige offered, stayed in the country for 27 years. Germany was not a unified country at this point in time and further railways were built in other states such as Saxony, where the Saxon State Railway opened in 1837 with a line from Dresden to Leipzig, and Prussia, where the Potsdam to Berlin line was opened in 1838.

Throughout the rest of Europe, railway development continued apace with railways opening in Belgium in 1835, Austria in 1837, the Netherlands in 1839 and Switzerland in 1844. In Italy railway development was, like Germany, severely restricted by the political structure of the country. It was also a country that was divided into many smaller states, each with their own borders. The first railway in Italy opened in October 1839, running between Naples and Portici, and, again in keeping with the German railway, it used Robert Stephenson & Company's 'Patentee' locomotives.

Scandinavia and Russia

The spread of railway technology from Europe to the rest of the world was initially a slow process. Apart from developments in the United States and Canada, there was little evidence of railway mania too far away from the birthplace of railways. In Scandinavia, Denmark was the first country to build a line, with the opening of the Baltic Line from Altona to Kiel in 1844. The climate and terrain of the region did not assist railway development, but lines opened in Norway in September 1854 and Sweden in December 1856.

The first railway in Russia ran from Pavlosk to Tsarskoe Selo, part of the St Petersburg & Pavlosk Railway. Mainly using horses for motive power, this line was built with a track gauge of six feet, although when the Moscow to St Petersburg line was constructed in 1851 that line utilised a 5ft gauge (1,524mm), which is still used throughout Russia to this day.

Above: George Stephenson, 'Father of the Railways', whose son, Robert, founded a locomotive building firm which became one of the biggest in 19th century England. The company continued to construct locomotives until the mid-1950s when it became part of GEC.

Left: At the opening of Italy's first railway line, between Naples and Portici, in 1839, crowds flocked to see the novel form of transportation. This painting by Salvatore Fergola (1799–c.1877) shows the train as its winds its way around the bay.

Right: This painting, by Abraham Solomon, entitled *The Meeting*, shows the interior of a first class carriage in the early 1800s.

Below: Before the railways, the usual method of public transportation was the stagecoach. This scene shows a coach and four, complete with rear mounted postillion. The posthorn he is holding was used to warn of the coach's approach.

THE COMING OF THE RAILWAYS was not greeted with universal enthusiasm. Before they became an accepted part of the landscape many commentators had predicted all manner of disastrous consequences if railways were built, ranging from children, animals and those of a nervous disposition being terrified, to smoke and fumes destroying the countryside. In the event, these fears proved to be groundless, and railways became accepted just as canals had been a century before. The public soon began to recognise the benefits of rail travel, not least in the reduction of journey times between large cities. When the Great Western Railway opened in 1841, the journey from London to Bristol took just over five hours. This was not only a saving in time, but it was also a great improvement in comfort, as, before the coming of the railway, a one or two-day journey taken in a horse-drawn carriage between these two cities was a tiring and uncomfortable experience, especially since horses had to be changed at regular intervals.

Passenger Comfort

In the early days, rail travel was still something of an adventure, especially in comparison with the facilities afforded to passengers after 1890. Much depended on the type of ticket a passenger was able to afford. Although first class travellers had the benefit of comfortable seats and windows with glass, there was no train heating and, as there were no corridors, they were locked in their compartments between

for every railway to run at least one third class train each day, with passengers being carried in 'covered carriages', at a rate of one penny a mile.

One further challenge on these early railways was finding something to eat. Restaurant cars were not introduced until the latter part of the 19th century and passengers took refreshment at stations en route. The quality of fare served was variable, at best. At Wolverton, on the London & Birmingham Railway the staff, comprising a female supervisor and 'seven young ladies', are said to have served hungry travellers with pork pies, buns, cakes and all manner of other delicious snacks. Elsewhere the food served was rather poorer. Isambard Kingdom Brunel wrote of the notorious refreshment rooms at Swindon, 'I avoid taking anything there if I can help it'.

Royal Approval

Railway travel was given the royal seal of approval when, in 1842, Queen Victoria made her first rail journey, from Slough to Paddington, finally making it respectable in the eyes of the middle classes. But it was not just those with money who benefited from the enormous revolution in travel that was brought by the railways. Even though many workers and their families could not afford to travel on normal services they could take advantage of the many excursions the railways ran. These allowed them the experience of visiting the sea or the countryside, something they would never have been able to do before the coming of the train.

Above: This picture shows the hustle and bustle of a typical 19th century busy railway terminus.

Below: In the early days of the railway many of the gentry had their own private railway coach. This is Queen Adelaide's, widow of William IV and aunt of Queen Victoria.

stations. At night, oil lamps were the only form of lighting.

Second class passengers fared less well. Seated in carriages with roofs but no windows, journeys, especially in winter, were a cold experience. If this was not bad enough, third class passengers travelled in completely open wagons fitted with seats, exposed to all weathers, not to mention the cinders, sparks and smoke from the locomotive.

Some railways were unwilling to carry third class passengers at all. Those that did, ran their trains at inconvenient times and were much slower than the first or second class services. It was not until a passenger froze to death in a GWR open carriage in Sonning Cutting, near Reading, that the British government stepped in to assist the third class traveller. Gladstone's *Railway Act* of 1844 made it mandatory

THE OPENING UP OF CONTINENTS

Above: This picture shows two typical American wood-burning 4–4–0 passenger locomotives of the 1860s. The locomotive on the left is unusual in that it is an inside cylinder 4–4–0, of which few were built in America. The machine on the right is a conventional American bar-framed 4–4–0 with outside cylinders and connecting rods, of which many thousands were built.

North America

IN THE YEARS BEFORE the Civil War, America experienced something of its own 'railway mania' as large numbers of railways were built in states up and down the east coast including lines towards the Mississippi, Missouri and Ohio rivers, with routes from New York to Lake Erie, Richmond to Memphis and Baltimore to St Louis.

The Transcontinental Railway

The railways offered both government and settlers the opportunity to open up vast tracts of land which the former wanted to develop and in which the latter wanted to establish a new life. The key to the unlocking of this immense resource was the mighty task of constructing a transcontinental railway, conceived in the midst of the Civil War. President Lincoln was concerned with the isolation of the west coast states and so, in 1862, the Pacific Railroad Bill was passed.

It wasn't until the end of the war, in 1865, that construction was begun by two companies – in the East, the Union Pacific and in the West, the Central Pacific. Both railroads were given generous financial incentives to complete the project. They were given 10 miles (16km) of land in alternate strips each side of the line, plus loans of up to $48,000 per mile.

Shortages of labour were common, and so cheap Chinese workers were drafted in. Extremes of weather hampered progress; including drought, storms, blizzards and avalanches which were compounded by attacks from Native Indian tribes who were, understandably, reluctant to relinquish their ancestral lands.

It was thought that the 1,780-mile (2,864km) line might take over 10 years to build, but it was completed in just four. The two companies finally met at Promontory Point, Utah on 10 May 1869. Following the lines across prairie, desert and mountain had been another new invention, the telegraph, and so when the last ceremonial gold-plated final spike was driven in, the operator was able to send the message, "Done!".

Land Grant Railroads

In tandem with the construction of the transcontinental railway other lines pushed out into the prairies. Companies such as the Chicago & North Western, the Burlington, and Rock Island railroads were all given generous parcels of land by the US government from which they could profit in return for the construction of lines. As well as these 'land grant railroads', three further transcontinental railways had been driven across America by 1890 – the Southern Pacific, the Northern Pacific and the Atchison, Topeka & Santa Fe. Such was the growth of railway development in the USA that by this date, route mileage exceeded 163,500 miles (263,000km), compared with just over 9,000 miles (14,400km) 40 years before.

Africa

In Africa, railways were largely developed by the colonial activities of European powers such as Britain, France, Belgium and Germany. These left the continent with a series of lines linking the coast and the interior. The boldest scheme of all was that put forward by Cecil Rhodes who proposed a 'Cape to Cairo' railway that was to run north to south through Africa joining up the British colonies. The First World War ended this dream and the line never progressed further north than Rhodesia (now Zimbabwe). In South Africa, Rhodes was again involved when Dutch and British interests competed to build the first railway to link the gold mining areas of Witwatersrand with the coast. In the event, the British Cape Government Railway, under Rhode's leadership, reached Johannesburg in September 1892.

Central and South America

The development of railways in Latin America was a complex process. The railways of Mexico are perhaps untypical of the rest of the continent, its large network built largely between 1880 and 1900, was engineered and financed mainly by the USA. The Panama Railroad, opened in 1855, was built to transport passengers and goods across the Central American isthmus, saving passengers a long and dangerous sea voyage around Cape Horn. In South America, railway building began later, but was again financed by European countries. Work was often hindered by the difficult terrain the railroads covered and the complex and sometimes unstable politics of the region.

Left: In 1880, Andrew Onderdonk, secured the contracts for the construction of 128 miles of rail between Yale and Savona, at the west end of Kamloops Lake, BC, Canada. This picture, taken in the lower Fraser Valley, shows Onderdonk's track layers carrying sleepers from the supply train.

Below: The railway in Uganda, commenced in 1891, was built through previously unpenetrated jungle. The embankment approach to this bridge was built up by local people who carried the spoil in head baskets.

Right: A Caledonian express headed by a small 4–4–0. Note the carriage truck behind the locomotive tender; these were a common sight on express trains until World War I.

Below: The first railway in Japan opened in 1872. This 19th century print shows the train in Shimbashi station, Tokyo. The locomotives and equipment used on this railway were all built in England.

Britain

IN MARCH 1899 the Great Central Railway, the last major railway project of the Victorian age, finally opened for business. This event effectively ended nearly 75 years of furious railway development in Britain, which had begun with the opening of the Stockton & Darlington Railway in 1825. From 1850 to 1900, early lines, such as the Liverpool & Manchester, London & Birmingham, and Great Western, were consolidated or absorbed by new or existing companies. Many new lines had been proposed and built, and by 1900 Britain's railway network was, apart from some minor additions later, at its greatest extent. Few settlements of any significance did not have a railway station – in many cases two. Inter-company rivalry, which had its roots in the 'railway mania' period also meant that there was duplication of routes between many cities. Railways had become the main mode of transport for most people, and were untroubled by the spectre of road competition.

New Technology

Improvements in technology in the period made rail travel faster, safer and more comfortable. Locomotive design evolved rapidly, from the 2–2–2 wheel arrangement designs common in 1850, through to the fast and powerful 4–4–0 engines used by many British railways at the turn of the century. Important though speed was, breakthroughs in signalling and safety were just as significant. The adoption of better braking, such as the Westinghouse system, prompted by accidents like the one at Armagh in 1889 and subsequent government legislation, increased public confidence in railways. Better signalling also assisted this process, with the introduction of inventions including the block telegraph system and the interlocking of points and signals.

Another advance was the resolution of the 'Gauge Question' that had caused much debate and argument. In 1850, a Royal Commission ruled in favour of the adoption of a national track gauge measuring 4ft 8½in (1,432mm). This dealt a severe blow to Isambard Kingdom Brunel's Great Western Railway that had been built to a gauge of 7ft (2,436mm). The GWR began modifying their track in the early 1870s, a task that was to last until May 1892, when the last section from Paddington to Penzance was finally converted.

Europe

In the rest of Europe, the consolidation of the railway systems of each country was matched by a gradual linking of all these lines into Europe-wide network. For the rich, travel by rail

across the continent was best done by trains operated by the Wagons–Lits company, which had been set up by a Belgian, Georges Nagelmackers. He not only inaugurated the 'Orient Express', but also trains such as the 'Calais–Nice–Rome Express' and the 'Sud Express', which linked Paris with Madrid and Lisbon. This luxury travel was very different from the less salubrious European trains where average speeds were no more than 30mph (48kph). In Germany, railway development was stifled by the political structure of the country until the unification of German States by Bismarck in 1871, after which track mileage almost doubled.

Asia

In Russia, the railway network grew slowly. In 1850 there were only 108 miles (174km) of track, while 20 years later this had risen to over 5,000 miles (8,000km). In the next three decades a great surge of building took place, so that by 1900 there were over 27,000 miles (43,400km) of track, much of it part of the great Trans–Siberian Railway, on which work started in 1891 and was completed almost a decade later. Japan opened its first railway in 1872. This was relatively late in comparison with many other countries but it caught up fast, and by 1890 had more than 1,500 miles (2,400km) of track. By 1900, few parts of the world had not seen the benefits of railways, and where development had started early, it was now well established. Elsewhere, such as in African and South American colonial areas, embryonic networks were planned or under construction.

Великій Сибирскій путь.—Grand Chemin de la Sibérie. № 3.
Мостъ черезъ р. Ушайку.

Above: A pair of O Class 0–8–0 Tender locomotives on a mixed train standing on a viaduct on the Trans-Siberian Railway *c.*1898. The O Class locomotives were some of the most numerous designs produced in Russia, both before and after the 1917 Revolution.

BY THE END OF THE 19th century, the revolutionary impact that railways had made on the world had become fully apparent and their use as a form of mass communication was firmly established. Although the less glamorous goods business made railway companies more money, it was the advances made in the running of express passenger trains that caught the imagination of the travelling public. Many advances could be linked to refinements and improvements in the construction of locomotives, rolling stock and track. As well as more powerful engines, express trains also had much better carriages, which had corridors, restaurant cars, toilets and heating, something that had been conspicuously absent previously.

Competing for Custom

Competition between railway companies also improved services with railways striving to run ever faster trains than their rivals. In Britain, many towns and cities had at least two railways serving them. Both the Great Western Railway and the London & North Western Railway ran trains from London to Birmingham, and, in the years before World War I, competed to provide a two-hour express from the Capital.

In the USA distances run by trains were much larger, but the competition was no less fierce. The New York to Chicago route pitted the New York Central Railroad and the Pennsylvania Railroad against each other. In 1902 the latter managed to reduce the journey time of its 'Pennsylvania Special' express down to 20 hours.

Serving the Commuter

Railways were also instrumental in changing the geography of cities and towns by the introduction of suburban services. Around large conurbations networks of lines spread inexorably outwards, enabling people to travel longer distances to and from work. As cities as diverse as Berlin, Calcutta, Johannesburg and Sydney became ever more polluted and clogged with traffic, so commuters travelled from further away. Railways not only served suburban areas, but also created them, with dormitory settlements springing up around the new lines. Improvements in rolling stock experienced by long distance travellers were not passed on to commuters whose trains were often cramped and uncomfortable.

Until the middle of the 20th century, steam locomotives were used to run commuter services until they were replaced by new diesel or electric services. Passengers who had choked in smokey tunnels, such as those built by the Metropolitan and District lines in London had previously found the novelty of electric traction much more to their liking. In America's cities, urban elevated railroads were built, run initially by steam, but soon converting to electricity. Chicago led the way in 1895, followed quickly by Boston and Philadelphia, with New York opening its first 'El' line in 1904.

Branch Lines

Away from the grime and bustle of cities, railway companies ran less well patronised and much slower branch line trains. Whereas suburban trains made frequent stops at stations that were very close, branch lines linked rural settlements, often many miles apart. An integral part of the landscape through which they ran, most were uneconomical from the day they opened, having been promoted by, and for, local people. Train speeds were often low, rarely exceeding 20mph (32kph) and ample time was built into timetables to allow station staff to gossip with train crews and passengers!

Although operated at a leisurely pace, these lines could also sometimes perform the important task of enabling city dwellers to have access to fresh produce such as milk, vegetables and fruit, which could be moved into towns very quickly. The Great Western's Cheddar Valley line was famous for its strawberry traffic, while others were important for less glamorous, but no less wholesome produce, such as potatoes or broccoli. Quite how important branch lines were to the communities they served has only become apparent in recent years, with rural areas denied any form of transport but the private car.

Left: London North Western express, at London Euston. Piloted by a Webb Jumbo 2–4–0, the second locomotive is a Prince of Wales Class 4–6–0.

Below: Although, by the early 1840s, local newspapers were publishing timetables, it was some time before printed timetables became available. One of the first was *The Intelligible Railway Guide*, which was published in 1858.

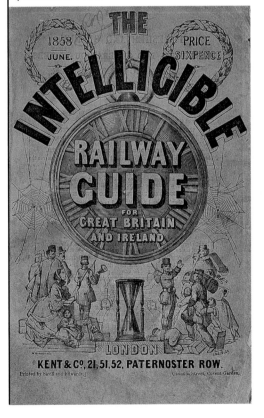

GREAT BRITAIN – EMPIRE AND EXPORTS

Above: **The stone bridge near Arrah on the East Indian Railway, c.1860.**

AS THE BIRTHPLACE OF RAILWAYS, it was only logical that British technology and expertise should provide the impetus for railway building all over the world. Many of Europe's and the New World's first lines used British locomotives, especially Stephenson 'Patentee' 2–2–2 designs, which ran all over the globe. British colonial power, the efforts of British railway locomotive and rolling stock manufacturers, and British companies running railways abroad, all ensured that British railway technology spread far from its roots.

India

In the process of developing its empire in the 19th century, Britain made considerable use of railways, enabling them to open up large areas of territory. As well as having economic and social importance, colonial railways were also strategic assets, and many were built to military standards. Some of the earliest colonial railways were constructed in India, where the first line opened between Bombay and Thana in 1853. The network was slow to expand, and some historians argue that if more railways were built at the time of the army mutiny of 1857, its effects would have been much reduced. Under the influence of one of its Governor-Generals, Lord Dalhousie, the subcontinent acquired one of the best planned networks in the empire. The network grew steadily. By 1870 major routes like Delhi–Calcutta and Bombay–Calcutta, over a 1,000 miles (1,600km) apart in each case, were linked and in 1880 the network totalled over 9,000 miles (14,400km). By the time of Indian independence in 1947, this had grown to over 34,000 miles (57,400km).

Africa

British influence in Africa extended beyond Cecil Rhode's 'Cape to Cairo' dream. Lines were built deep into the tropical heartland of Africa, with much development taking place in the period 1880–1920. One example was the system built in what was then called the Gold Coast, now Ghana. Over 500 miles (800km) of 3ft 6in gauge (1,067mm) lines were constructed to facilitate the movement of manganese, cocoa and timber from the interior. Tremendous engineering difficulties were overcome in the construction of the line with native uprisings and tropical diseases all taking their toll on the work force. Locomotives and rolling stock used on the line came from firms such as the Vulcan Foundry and Metro Cammell Ltd.

Australia

One final outpost that benefited from the development of railways was Australia. Lines grew in a rather piecemeal way, and although 3ft 6in gauge was favoured, the various states in the country did not choose one uniform gauge with 5ft 3in (1,600mm) and 4ft 8½in (1,432mm) also being used.

British Exporters

As well as exporting their products all over the world right from the earliest days of railway building, British railway manufacturers also benefited greatly from the construction of railways in British colonial territories. Firms such as the Vulcan Foundry, which dated back to 1830, with its factory at Newton-le-Willows in Lancashire, Beyer Peacock in Manchester, Hunslet of Leeds and North British in Scotland, all supplied to markets far beyond Great Britain. British influence abroad was far wider than just parts of the empire. The opening up of railways in South America owes much to the activities of British railway companies who constructed lines all over the continent. One of the largest private railways in Argentina was the Buenos Aires Great Southern Railway, which had over 5,000 miles (8,000km) of track. Another British owned concern was the Buenos Great Western Railway that had a 1,000-mile (1,600km) network. In Chile the two main railway companies, the Antofagasta Railway and the Nitrate Railway Company, were both British owned. Not surprisingly, many of the locomotives and rolling stock used on all these lines were built by British companies such as Beyer Peacock, Sentinel and the Yorkshire Engine Company.

Left: Built in 1879, the Siliguri to Darjeeling must be the most remarkable mountain railway in the world. Here we see a train rounding 'Agony Point', one of the four spirals on the line which allows the train to gain height in a short distance. The painting depicts one of two Beyer Garratt locomotives supplied to the Darjeeling line in the early 1900s. Both of these locomotives represented the third batch of Garratt locomotives supplied to any railway in the world and were usually only used in the flat plain section of this line.

Below: Probably one of the most unusual railways to be found anywhere in the British Empire was the Listowel & Ballybunion Railway, a monorail designed on the Latauge system which was first used on esparto grass railways in French North Africa. The company had a bizarre make-up in that it was owned by an English concern, designed by a Frenchman, built by a German engineer and operated in Ireland.

Above: An outside frame Baldwin 4–6–0, No. 43, owned by the Brazilian National Railways and working on part of their metre gauge network of rural lines. It is seen here hauling a cattle train at night.

Right: A Baldwin export 2–8–0, built to metre gauge, in use on a plantation line in Brazil *c.*1975. Note the balloon stack chimney which incorporates a spark arresting mechanism preventing sparks from igniting the sugar cane.

IN THE EARLY YEARS OF RAILWAYS, it was the British companies who dominated the export market. However, as the 19th century progressed, so other companies, particularly those from the United States, began to sell locomotives to many other countries. American practice showed itself to be quite different early on, with the adoption of bar frames instead of plate frames and 'hay-stack' fireboxes, with ruggedness of design also being a common characteristic.

The evolution of American locomotive design had much to do with the operating conditions they had to cope with in the 19th century. Trains ran long distances and had to be easy to overhaul and repair, since workshops were few and far between. This meant that although American–built engines were not the prettiest, they were reliable, powerful and easy to maintain.

South America

Engines built for export varied greatly in size, from small tank locomotives to large articulated types, with the 2–6–0, 2–8–0, 2–8–2 and 2–10–2 wheel arrangements being favoured. Initially, American engines were exported to countries with which the USA had contacts, such as Canada and Mexico, and later, farther afield to South America, Australia and New Zealand. In South America a variety of different locomotives were supplied of which two examples will illustrate the differing types. In 1933

the Baldwin Locomotive Company supplied the Colombian National Railways with an articulated 2–8–8–2 tank engine. Although only built for a 3ft gauge (914mm) line, the engine still weighed in at 128 tons. Three years later, Baldwin built a number of four-cylinder 2–8–2 tank locomotives for a railway in Chile. These were put into service on a metre gauge (3ft 3in) rack system that worked up to an altitude of 12,000 feet (3,600m).

India and South Africa

American locomotive builders also managed to penetrate markets traditionally dominated by the British, such as the colonial railways in India and

South Africa. In India, one of the most distinctive and attractive locomotives built by an American firm was the Indian Railways WP class 4–6–2, constructed by the Baldwin Locomotive Company in 1947. In the following 20 years Baldwin supplied over 750 of this streamlined Pacific type, which had replaced earlier British designs.

In South Africa, American designs began to appear fairly early. In 1891 the Cape Government Railways bought two Baldwin 2–6–0s to compare them with British locomotives, and, six years later, six 4–4–2 tank locomotives were bought from the same company for passenger work. When South African Railways were created their Locomotive Superintendent, D. A. Hendrie, purchased various engines from both the American Locomotive Company (Alco) and Baldwin. One of these was the first Mallet articulated type engine to run in South Africa – a 2–6–6–0 that was delivered in 1910. Colonel F. R. Collins, who replaced Hendrie in 1922, realised that conditions in South Africa were very similar to the United States, with long distance lines, steep gradients and primitive servicing facilities making American locomotive practice more suited to South Africa than the less robust British designs. With this in mind, he ordered numerous 4–8–2 and 4–6–2 locomotives from Alco and Baldwin.

Russia

Other more unlikely sources for American business were countries such as Russia, which, during World War I, ordered 1,200 5ft gauge 2–10–0 locomotives from US locomotive builders. There were only another 200 to be delivered before the Revolution prevented any further import. However, in 1944 a further 2,000 similar engines were supplied from the same source.

American Influence

In the years between the two world wars, America's firms also found their designs being copied and manufactured by other countries. The 'Josef Stalin' class 2–8–4 passenger locomotives, built in the Soviet Union in the 1930s, were American in all but name. As indeed were the engines constructed after World War II in China. Built with the assistance of Soviet engineers, these also bore the hallmarks of America's locomotives.

Below: An advertisement from the 1870s for the products of the Rogers Locomotive Machine Works, New York. The vignette shows an American type 4–4–0 locomotive.

Rogers Locomotive and Machine Works, of PATERSON, N. J. *New York Office:* 44 EXCHANGE PLACE.
Manufacturers of
LOCOMOTIVE ENGINES AND TENDERS.
AND OTHER RAILROAD MACHINERY.
J. S. ROGERS, Pres't,
R. S. HUGHES, Sec'y,
WM. S. HUDSON, Sup't,
} PATERSON, N. J.
ROBT. S. HUGHES Treas.
44 Exchange Place New York.
Poor's Manual of Railroads, 1879.

THE PREMIER FORM OF TRANSPORT

The Effects of World War I

The period of certainty and dominance enjoyed by railways before 1914 were brought to an abrupt end when war broke out in Europe. Until the outbreak of the conflict they had enjoyed something of a 'Golden Age'. After 1918, the certainty that railways were the profitable premier form of transport was gone for ever. Although the years before the Second World War are often seen as a glamorous and exciting, with railway, and in particular steam, development at its height, the images of prestigious express services such as the 'Flying Scotsman' and the 'Twentieth Century Limited', hid more difficult times for railways of the era. In the years immediately after the First World War, railways faced pressing problems. The most obvious was that countries involved in the conflict, particularly Belgium, France and Germany, either had railway networks damaged or destroyed by the war itself, or, as in Britain, had huge backlogs of maintenance and investment.

Road Transport

To railway management, however, it was the more widespread use of road transport that worried them most. With the end of the war, many servicemen returned home having been trained as drivers. This, with the availability of ex-army lorries and other vehicles, meant that the railway companies' grasp on goods traffic was less tight. The ability of lorries to deliver door to door compared with the somewhat antiquated goods system still used by the railways did not help either. The introduction of more widespread coach services also ate into railway passenger profits.

Reorganisation

The multiplicity of routes and lines in many countries led to changes in the ways railways were organised. In Britain, the 123 pre-war companies were amalgamated in 1923 into what became known as the 'Big Four': the Great Western, the London Midland & Scottish, the London & North Eastern and the Southern Railways. Although there were calls to nationalise railways elsewhere, it was only in Canada and Germany that this was fully carried out. The difficult times suffered by railways after the Great War were compounded by the 'Wall Street Crash' financial disaster, but railways responded to their difficulties in the best way they could, by introducing new trains and services to compete with their rivals. So began a period that saw some of the most glamorous and exciting developments. Railways became much more adept at publicising themselves, something which some companies, notably the Great Western Railway, had already begun to address before the war. In the 1920s and 1930s the publicity departments of all the large railways battled to create what we would now call a 'corporate image' for their companies.

Shaped for Speed

It was the new train services that caught the public imagination. Train speeds increased throughout the period, helped by further developments in locomotive design. Famous names such as Gresley, Collett and Stanier in Britain, Chapelon in France, and Woodard in the United States, designed powerful locomotives to run high-speed passenger services, but it was the introduction of streamlining which was probably the most significant development in this period.

The first streamlined trains were introduced in the United States; both the Union Pacific and the Burlington railroads running diesel powered trains from 1934 onwards. Virtually all the world's major railways introduced streamlined locomotives or trains of one sort or another. In Britain, Gresley-designed A4 class Pacifics hauled crack LNER expresses like the 'Silver Jubilee', and it was No. 4468 *Mallard* of this class, which broke the world speed record for steam locomotives in 1937 at 126mph (203 kph). Other examples of this development include the New York Central's Hudson 4–6–4s used on the 'Twentieth Century Limited' expresses; Class 05 4–6–4s, built by the Reichsbahn in Germany; and the 4–8–4 locomotives run by the Canadian National Railway. The streamline era may not have been the last chapter of the steam railway age, but after the 1930s, its dominance would never be the same.

2 *From* **Early Oddities** *to* **High Tech Wonders**

Richard Trevithick

In the years following the evolution of wagonways and early horse-worked tramroads of various gauges, came a period of rapid change and development. In the 1780s Thomas Newcomen and James Watt developed low pressure beam engines for pumping water out of mines, and, by the 1790s, Richard Trevithick, a Cornishman, had designed and built his high pressure road and rail engines – machines that changed the course of transport history.

Three of the earliest important rail-borne engines are the Coalbrookdale locomotive, built at Ironbridge, Shropshire, in 1803; the Pen-y-Darren Tramroad locomotive of 1804, which ran on an industrial tramway near Merthyr Tydfil, Glamorganshire, South Wales; and *Catch-Me-Who-Can*, which was demonstrated near Euston, London, in 1808, and had a single, vertical cylinder driving from the rear.

Most of Trevithick's locomotives were geared drive with front or rear single cylinders and smooth wheels that ran on flanged plateway rails. Although the locomotives in themselves were a success they were, however, let down by the poor quality of these wrought-iron fishbelly rails that kept breaking.

The Middleton Locomotives of 1812

One of the first successful uses of locomotives in industry was on the Middleton Railway, Leeds, in 1812. Designed by John Blenkinsop, these geared rack locomotives, which had two vertical cylinders, ran on strong cast-iron edge rails with, on one side, a rack section that secured the locomotive's adhesion.

Puffing Billy

William Hedley's 0–4–0 *Puffing Billy* of 1813 was an advance in design being driven through a single crank on one side. Because of bad track, it was rebuilt as an 0–8–0, then reverted to an 0–4–0 when the rail used was replaced with improved material.

George Stephenson

In 1815 George Stephenson designed and built an 0–4–0 locomotive for the Killingworth Colliery Railway, Northumberland. This machine ran on

flanged wheels, driven through two vertical cylinders with chain drive between the axles. In 1825 the Stock-ton & Darlington Railway opened to traffic with *Locomotion No. 1*, also designed and built by Stephenson, which was also driven through two vertical cylinders, but this time with a rear crank axle. *Locomotion* was followed in 1827 by Stephenson's 0–6–0 *Royal George*, both engines having a primitive form of 'boxpock' wheel, with holes, rather than spokes.

Early Exports from Britain

The development of the water tube boiler and plate and bar frames led to a new era in locomotive design, which in turn led to the shape of the steam locomotive we all recognise today. This design ran through the Stephenson 'Planet' 2–2–0 and 'Samson' type 0–4–0, one of which, *John Bull*, was the second British locomotive to be exported to the USA.

There were other designs that pushed locomotive to the edges of contemporary technology. These examples included Forester's 2–2–0 of 1834 for the Dublin & Kingstown Railway, the Bury-designed bar-framed 0–4–0, and the 2–2–0 locomotives which were built for both Britain and the USA.

The traffic in locomotives was not at all one way. The Norris Works in Philadelphia, Pennsylvania produced some notable 4–2–0 type locomotives for Britain's Birmingham & Gloucester Railway. Some of this type were built under licence by British builders such as Hick Hargreaves and James Nasmyth.

Brunel's Broad Gauge

On the Great Western, Isambard Kingdom Brunel opted for a gauge of 7ft (2.13m). Early broad gauge locomotives ranged from Stephenson's *North Star* to Daniel Gooch's *Fire Fly* and the *Iron Duke*. When they were built, the latter were the fastest locomotives in the world with an average speed of 50mph (80kph). The broad gauge came an end in 1892 when, over a weekend, the final mileage was converted to the standard gauge of 4ft 8in (1.46m).

Above: Catch-Me-Who-Can, Richard Trevithick's experimental locomotive which ran in 1808 on a circular railway behind a fence at Euston Square, London.

Below: This working replica of George Stephenson's *Locomotion No. 1* was built in 1975.

THE BASIC LOCOMOTIVE FORM EMERGES

Right: A former British-owned Buenos Aires Great Southern Railway Bayer Peacock 4–6–0, built *c.*1910. It is seen here, sold out of service, shunting military stores at a naval base.

Below: A 0–8–0 heavy goods locomotive built for the Turkish State Railways by Anciens Establishment Cail, France, in 1906.

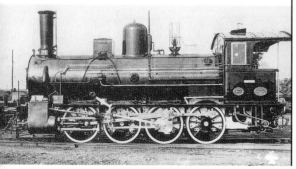

Second Generation Locomotive Development

After the establishment of the 2–2–2, the 2–2–0 and 0–4–0, a further development took place as the result of the increase in weight and length of trains. Most of the major railways in Europe, the Middle East, Australia and the Far East ordered, or built, 2–4–0 tank and tender locomotives for express and branch line work. In Britain and Ireland 75 per cent of companies had locomotives of this wheel arrangement on top link and semi-fast trains. Two notable examples, introduced in the 1870s, were the Midland Railway Kirtley 2–4–0s and the Francis Webb designed LNWR 'Jumbo' 2–4–0s.

As the 0–6–0 tender and tank types were used for both goods and passenger trains they survived until the end of steam traction all over the world. Two examples of this type were, in Britain, the standard LMS 3F 'Jinty' tank and, in Pakistan, the SGS class tender type.

Although the 4–2–2 was a British wheel arrangement, examples were built for export including a batch built for China just before World War I. These were later re-built as 4–4–0 tender locomotives.

Both the Great Western and Great Eastern railways had classes of 4–2–2 express tender locomotive on top link work from the 1890s until World War I. The Midland Railway 'Spinner' 4–2–2s were among some of the most elegant locomotives ever built, some lasting in traffic until the 1920s.

The 0–8–0 was a successful type, both in tank and tender form and was used by many railways around the world, notably Germany, where the Prussian State Railways had large numbers of G10 and G8 class tender locomotives. In Britain, the Great Northern Railway had 'Long Tom' 0–8–0 tender locomotives and the Sturrock 0–8–0 tanks, which were used for suburban train services. The LNWR had the famous 'Bill Bailey' and G2 class 0–8–0 goods tender locomotives.

Developments in America and Europe

In Europe, most of the large private and state railways were building and using 4–4–0s until quite late. Of particular interest were the Midland and LMS compound 4–4–0s, with high and low pressure cylinders, which were built into the early 1930s, and the Southern Railway 'Schools' class built in the 1930s which were the most powerful of the type. The last 4–4–0s in the world, the VS class, were built in Britain for the Great Northern Railway of Ireland in 1949.

With the advent of faster trains there was yet again a need for even larger express locomotives. This led, in the early 20th century, to the 4–4–2 Atlantic type which was used in large numbers in America and Europe. In America the Pennsylvania and Reading railroads, the main users of this type of locomotive, operated them on the first truly express passenger services. Other American companies had 'Camelback' versions of the type, with their cabs above the boiler, the last ones not being withdrawn until the early 1950s. The last working Atlantics in the world, on the Caminhos de Ferro de Moçambique, were withdrawn in 1975.

The next developments were the 4–6–0 and the 4–6–2 Pacific types. First built in America in the 1890s, within ten years they had found favour in Western and Central Europe. In Britain the Great Western and LNWR were at the forefront of locomotive design and development but other companies were not too far behind. Two notable examples of European 4-6-0 were the Great Western 'Castle' class, which was in production from 1923 until 1951, and the Prussian-built P8 class which were built in large numbers in Germany, Poland and Romania from 1908 until the 1920s.

The French engineer, Chapelon rebuilt and designed some efficient examples of this type, the most famous of all being the 2–3–1E (4–6–2) which lasted well into the 1960s.

Sir Nigel Gresley's A1/A3 class Pacifics for the LNER, together with the famous A4 streamlined engines, were outstanding from the 1920s to the 1960s. Another prominent British designer was William Stanier of the LMS who produced the beautiful 'Princess Royals' and 'Princess Coronations', which remained in service until the mid-1960s.

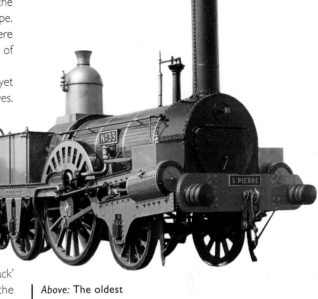

Above: **The oldest surviving French locomotive is No. 33** *Saint Pierre.* **Built in 1844 for the Paris–Rouen Railway, it is now preserved in the French Railway Museum at Mulhouse.**

Above: This oil-burning Henschel-built four cylinder compound 4–6–0 was designed, *c.*1912, for use on the Baghdad railway. Despite being built in Germany, it still owes a great deal to French design.

Below: This LMS, Fowler version, compound No. 1112, built in 1926, is the best example of a British locomotive of the type. Its strong rugged construction, with a thermally efficient boiler, valve gear and cylinders of a sophisticated design, allowed it to provide a powerful and efficient tractive effort.

THE COMPOUND DESIGN, using high and low pressure cylinders resulted from the need for greater tractive effort, but had a mixed fortune on the railways of the world where used, principally in Britain and mainland Europe.

USA

Although American engineers built prototypes in small batches, or as one-offs, they largely decided that larger, simple expansion types were more in keeping with their needs. The only notable exception was the period from the 1890s until the 1920s, when most of the larger American railways built, or ordered, Mallet compound heavy freight locomotives, of which some lasted into the mid-1950s.

Britain

Francis Webb of the LNWR built some early examples of compound locomotives including the 'Greater Britain' 2–2–2–2, of which one was built under licence for the Pennsylvania Railroad. Webb also built some 2–2–2 compounds with a similar look to the 'Jumbo' 2–4–0s. These, together with the 2–2–2–2 tank types, the 4–4–0 'Jubilee' class, and some 0–8–0 goods engines, made up a sizeable number of locomotives on the LNWR.

On the Midland Railway, Richard Deeley successfully designed and built some fine 4–4–0 compounds that were later rebuilt. Further examples were added under Henry Fowler for the Midland and LMS. However, quite unlike Webb on the LNWR, the Midland Railway used the 4–4–0 types almost exclusively for express work. Other British railway companies that experimented with compounds were the North Eastern, London & South Western, and the Great Western.

France

Most French railway companies developed their locomotive strategy from British technology, the two main early types being the Buddicom 2–2–2 and the Crampton 4–2–0 singles. From the 1870s

there was considerable interest in compounding in so far as the Ouest Railway bought a Webb 2–2–2. By the early 1900s the French companies had large groups of compounds 4–4–0, 4–6–0 and Atlantic types.

An important time in the development of the compounds was the period 1900 to 1914, with de Glehn 4–4–2 and 4–6–0 types and du Bousquet 4–6–2 and Pacific type locomotives. It was, however, the development by Chapelon in the 1920s and '30s that advanced the scientific concept of compounding to its ultimate. Chapelon at first re-built some average Pacifics and 4–8–0 tender locomotives owned by the Paris Orleans, Midi, Paris-Lyons-Mediterranee and Etat railway compa-nies. The result was a radical improvement in drafting and thermal efficiency, which in turn led to the construction of a 2–12–0 A1, rebuilt from a 6,000 class of 1909, which was outshopped in June 1940.

No further development occurred until after World War II when a whole new group of classes of steam locomotives was planned. This project was cancelled, but not before the construction of

4–8–4 A1, a rebuild from an Etat 4–8–2. The most outstanding Chapelon locomotives were the 2–3–1 G class Pacifics, built new in 1938, and the 1–4–1 TC class tanks, which had Gosard valve gear, built for Nord suburban passenger services in the late 1930s.

Karl Gölsdorf

In Austria, Karl Gölsdorf was tackling similar prob-lems to the French engineers but attempted a solution by a different route. His compound locomotives benefited from improved steam cir-culation, hence the double domed arrangement. There were various 4–6–0, 4–4–2 and 2–8–0 classes that became standard throughout the Austro-Hungarian Empire. The Gölsdorf improve-ments were subject to further developments by Stumpf in Germany who further experimented with drafting improvements and the Uniflow sys-tem of steam circulation with which a number of railways in Britain and Europe experimented from the late 1890s.

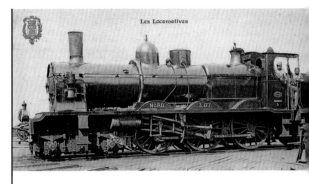

Above: A French Nord 4–6–0 compound c.1910, designed to the de Glehn principle for use as a mixed traffic locomotive. These survived in service until the mid-1950s on the SNCF.

VERTICAL BOILERS

THE DESIGN AND USE OF VERTICAL-boilered locomotives date from the early days of railways. In 1830 the Baltimore & Ohio line put into service Peter Cooper's 0–4–0 *Tom Thumb,* on the 13-mile (21km) stretch between Baltimore and Ellicott's Mill. Although this was more of a scientific model than a proper locomotive it did convince American business that steam traction was not simply a flash in the pan but a practical alternative to horse-drawn transport.

J. P. de Winton

One of the early builders of vertical boilered locomotives was J. P. de Winton's Union Works in Caernarfon, North Wales. De Winton's engines were designed specifically for the narrow gauge slate quarry railways that ranged from 1ft 11½in to 3ft gauge (600mm to 914mm). De Winton's engines were very robust and well suited to the rough tracks and sharp curves of the lines for which they were intended.

Sentinel

Possibly the best-known builder of vertical boilered locomotives was Sentinel of Shrewsbury. The company opened for business in 1906 constructing principally steam road vehicles, however, in 1923 their patent steam unit was incorporated into the first Sentinel-Cammell rail car. At the same time the unit was applied for use in shunting and light goods traffic locomotives. Sentinel built 870 power units of this type before ceasing production in 1957. Among the designs produced were a variety of 0–4–0VB type locomotives for main line company and industrial use, both for Britain, notably the LNER and LMSR, and for export. One was sold to the Leopoldina Railway in Brazil. This remarkable engine was used as an inspection car with a day saloon and pantry at one end, and bathroom and sleeping accommodation at the other. With the boiler in the centre, the coach could be driven from either end. Other examples of Sentinel locomotives, many of which were used for shunting and departmental use, found their way to places as far apart as France, Denmark, Sweden, Egypt, South Africa, India, Ceylon, Columbia, Australia, and New Zealand.

Other Builders

A development of the small 0–4–0 type vertical boiler locomotive was the steam tram engine that had a light railway and street tramway association. One builder who constructed such engines was Beyer Peacock of Manchester who, between 1881 and 1910, built 97 examples for the Javan Tramways. Henry Hughes of Loughborough was another builder of tram engines. In 1876 a tram fitted with one of his engines commenced running on the Leicester Tramways. Weighing about 4 tons the engine was equipped with a device for consuming its own smoke and condensing the steam – a stipulation of the *Tramways Act* of 1870. This was soon transferred to Govan where, in company with eight others, it worked until 1881, when they were replaced by new engines. Other similar engines were sold to various tramways including Bristol, Guernsey, Paris and Lille.

Continental Europe

Most main line companies around the world experimented with steam rail cars. On Continental Europe vertical boilered trams were built by Jung, Franco-Belge and Ventpun. Notable examples of vertical-boilered locomotives in use elsewhere in the world included those on the Swiss State Railways and the Bavarian State Railway. August Borsig of Berlin was a prolific builder for both the home market and export. One of their products, of standard gauge, is the world's last surviving steam tram. Built in 1910 it still works at the Tebicuary Sugar Mill in Paraguay, having formerly worked around the docks of Argentina's capital, Buenos Aires. The last tram engines in Europe were not withdrawn until the 1960s.

Above: Insular Lumber Company No. 7 hauling a train of logs over a timber trestle. This 0–6–6–0 Mallet compound was one of the last of its type in regular use anywhere in the world.

Below: A Fairlie 0–6–6–0 articulated locomotive, built in 1911 for the Mexican National Railway by the Vulcan Foundry. These oil-burners, used on main line sevices to haul heavy freight and mixed trains, survived in traffic until the late 1920s.

The Mallet

In the 1880s, with the development of Mallet artic-ulated locomotives in France, design went in a new direction. At first, these machines took the form of narrow gauge 0–4–4–0Ts, but later examples were built in all gauges, for both home and export. Some French main line railway companies experimented with, or ordered, complete classes of Mallets. One such was the Nord, which had about 40 of the type for use on freight trains. They were also used extensively on French minor railways, especially metre gauge networks in the various departments, examples being the Paris Orleans, Coreze, the Vivarais and the Reseau Breton.

North America

Although North American articulated locomotive development was taking a different direction with the design and production of a group of machines, such as the Shay, Climax, Hustler and Heisler, which were made for specialist and general use – mostly in the logging and mining industries. Main line and short line systems also used large Mallet and Meyer type locomotives from the 1890s and early 1900s.

At the end of the 19th century, the main line North American railways were looking at the potential of heavy Mallet locomotives for moving longer and heavier freight trains. Their use as banker, or helper, engines also looked promising. Some of the first railroads to benefit from their use were the Pennsylvania and Southern Pacific, who experimented with, and used in traffic, this new type of locomotive. Many companies, such as the Boston & Maine, Union Pacific and Norfolk & West-ern, had fleets of these machines, while the Southern Pacific built a fleet of cab-forward articu-lated locomotives to work through the tunnelled sections of main line in the west of the system.

The 'Challenger' and 'Big Boy' Giants

Later, in the 1940s, the Union Pacific developed the 'Challenger' and 'Big Boy' type articulated loco-

motives, which were used in the far west of the system to haul heavy freights over Sherman Hill. The 'Big Boys' lasted in traffic until 1960, while the Norfolk & Western's articulated A and Y6B type Mallets were the last large articulated locomotives in use in North America. Used to haul long coal trains and heavy freights between the Appalachians and Norfolk, Virginia, they were taken out of service in 1960.

The Meyer

From the mid-1880s, in Germany, as an alternative to the Mallet, the Meyer was perfected. These locomotives were built both for standard and narrow gauge lines, particularly the Royal Saxon State railways where there was an extensive rural minor railway network built to 760mm gauge (2ft 5½in). In Saxony these machines were also used on some standard gauge lines where they proved to be very successful. Standard gauge examples lasted until the late 1950s, while some are still in use on narrow gauge lines in the former East Germany.

The Garratt

In Britain, development took a new form with the design and development of the Kitson Meyer locomotives, mostly built for export to South America and the Colonies, and the Beyer Garratt, built by Beyer Peacock, which was used both at home, by the LMS and LNER, and overseas. Also, in the UK, two 0–4–4–0 industrial Garratts were supplied – one to the Vivian Copper Works, near Swansea, and the other to a colliery near Coventry. Probably the most famous Garratts ever built were the Class 59 2–8–4+4–8–2s that ran in Kenya on the East African Railways. The largest Garratt ever built was the one and only order for Russia in 1932. This giant locomotive was used for tests by the Leningrad Railway Institute and was later broken up for scrap.

The articulated locomotive era ended with the coming of the diesel and electric locomotives in mass numbers in the 1950s and 1960s. The Beyer Garratts were the last articulated locomotives to see traffic in South Africa, where the Class GL and GMAM types were used on heavy freight trains, and in Zimbabwe, where Classes 15, 16A and 20 and 20A Garratts are still to be seen working.

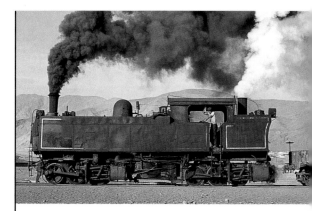

Above: The last working Kitson Meyer articulated locomotive on the former nitrate mining railway at Teltal, Chile. These locomotives were in great demand worldwide and large numbers were built before the advent of the Garratt which replaced them.

Above: The steam-hauled New York Elevated Railway, built upon steel pillars, ran through New York streets at various altitudes. Although it was generally above the house tops, in some places the track was level with second-storey windows.

Britain – Underground

The first underground railway was London's Metropolitan which opened on 10 January 1863. Until March 1869, it was mixed standard and broad gauge with conventional trains hauled by steam locomotives fitted with condensing apparatus. The railway was built by the 'cut and cover' method generally following the streets to avoid the foundations of buildings. In standard gauge form, it eventually extended through to the suburbs where it ran on the surface.

The first electric underground railway was also in London, the City & South London (C&SL), which opened on 18 December 1890. This became the nucleus of today's network of standard gauge lines using multiple unit stock with a low profile to fit the dimensions of the tube. The joint engineer was J. H. Greathead, who had developed the eponymous shield that enables deep tunnels, lined with brick or iron segments, to be made with greater speed and safety than most other methods. This was an important factor as the 'tube', as such lines became known, passed under the River Thames. The C&SL was not the first tube railway, for Greathead had been the assistant engineer to London's Tower Subway. This used cable traction, as did the 4ft gauge (1,219mm) Glasgow Subway which opened on 14 December 1896.

Europe – Underground

The twin city of Budapest claims to have had the first underground railway on mainland Europe. The Franz Joseph Electric Underground Railway, opened in May 1896, was standard gauge, 2.3 miles (3.7km) long and constructed on the 'cut and cover' method. Currently, one of the best ways to get around this busy city is by the much extended system. Those familiar with the Moscow underground will recognise the design of the rolling stock on one of the lines. The Moscow system, begun in 1932, is notable for the impressive and ornate architecture of some of the earlier stations. Early lines were 'cut and cover' but later ones were deep level tubes.

Paris was early in the field. Line 1 opened on 19 July 1900 and by the end of the year over 8 miles (12.5km) were in operation. Trains run in 'cut and cover' tunnels, wider than would be suggested by the first sight of the narrow-bodied stock. Testing of pneumatic-tyred stock began in 1951. The tyred bogie wheels run on concrete strips laid outside the conventional track while horizontal-tyred wheels guide the bogies. In the event of failure, the vehicle sinks onto normal bogie wheels mounted inboard of the tyred ones. In recent years, the Metro has been joined by an increasing number of heavy rail routes running in tunnels across the city. This has given the network the appearance of that of Berlin which, whilst operating trains that approach full loading gauge standards, it also has a complex network of underground and surface routes dating from 1910.

UNDERGROUND AND OVERHEAD RAILWAYS

Europe began the underground movement and it continues to expand with mixtures of light and heavy rail and automated systems. Early systems were also built in the USA, Canada, South America and Japan.

Britain – Overhead

Britain had the first electric overhead line, the Liverpool Overhead Railway, which started on 6 March 1893 and closed on 30 December 1956. It ran near the docks and above the streets feeding them.

USA – Overhead

Probably the best known overhead railway is the New York Elevated, the first section of which opened in 1870. The standard gauge steam line used small locomotives, including the unusual Forney type, to negotiate the very sharp curves as the lines followed the streets. The New York El was electrified in the early 1900s, some years after the Chicago Elevated in 1895.

Above: A London underground scene *c.*1950.

Left: London's Baker Street station as it appeared in the late 19th century. Notice that the broad gauge trains are still being steam hauled and the natural light vents from the roof, this was a feature of the first London undergound stations.

WORLD STANDARD DESIGNS

THE RAPID EVOLUTION and development of railways around the world, coupled with piecemeal construction, resulted in a lack of any standardisation of motive power. Varying locomotive requirements led to many differing designs being ordered from commercial locomotive builders and companies that built their own locomotives all had their own distinctive styles. In general, this applied throughout the steam age, although exceptions occurred with a few designs being produced in enormous numbers, particularly in the case of wartime engines.

India

Here, the emerging metre gauge networks used double-framed, outside-cylinder 0–6–0s introduced in 1884. Known as the F class, over 1,000 were built by at least a dozen builders, including works in Britain, Germany and India itself, with some engines seeing service in East Africa.

Russia

The most numerous type ever was the Russian E class 0–10–0 which was introduced in 1912. The heavy destruction of Russian railways during World War II meant extra locomotives were essential and further orders for Class Es were placed in Rumania, Czechoslovakia, Poland and Hungary, bringing the grand total built to upwards of 13,000. This outnumbered the famous Russian O class 0–8–0s produced between 1889 and 1923, of which some 9,000 were built.

Germany

Prussian State Railways produced a family of designs that also reached large numbers, albeit nothing so imposing as the Russians. Their P8 passenger class 4–6–0s numbered some 3,500 engines whilst the heavy freight G8 class 0–8–0 exceeded 5,000 examples. Both types saw wide-spread service in Europe as a result of the two world wars. In contrast, the larger Prussian 3-cylinder G12 class totalled 1,200 engines but the most famous German standard design however was the Kriegslok 2-10-0 built for military operations throughout Europe during World War II. A total of 6,300 of this

wartime austerity were constructed, and if this quantity is added to the standard Class 50, from which they were derived, the basic type numbered some 10,000 locomotives.

Other types built specifically for wartime operations assumed huge totals. The Feldbahn narrow gauge 0–8–0T, built for military field railways during World War I, ultimately reached several thousand examples from a wide variety of German builders – the type also being produced after the war as a standard industrial locomotive. Major Marsh's Class S160 2–8–0s of World War II, built in the USA to the British loading gauge as an alternative version of William Stanier's 8F class 2–8–0s, reached some 2,500 engines while the McArthur metre gauge Mikado 2–8–2, though not so numerous, saw use in Europe, Africa, India and the Far East.

USA

The archetypal American express passenger diesel locomotive was General Motor's standard passenger 6-axle 'E' cab design, built between 1937 and 1963. In 1939 the new 4-axle FT freight locomotive proved a great success and, with later F-units, did much to eliminate steam on American railroads. Competition caused EMD to develop units with full width cabs between narrower motor and equipment covers. These 'Hood' types gave better visibility for the driver and were a great deal easier to maintain. First sold in 1949 as General Purpose and 6-axle Special Duties versions, they are still being built today, with recent models incorporating new technology.

China

The combination of centralised control under communism and vast land masses rendered China the country with the greatest degree of standardisation. Until as recently as 1985, China had some 11,000 steam locomotives in service, 90 per cent of which could be accounted for by six basic types. The only steam locomotives still under construction are the industrial SY class 2-8-2s which, in 1997, totalled 1,700 engines. With building now almost complete these are unlikely to exceed the earlier JF class main line Mikado that was classically American in concept and totalled at least 2,500 examples coming from builders in America, Japan and China itself.

Above: An E Class main line passenger diesel. These were built in large numbers from the late 1930s and used on most A and B Class American railroads.

Left: China's standard QJ Class 2–10–2 is the world's most numerous steam type, with at least 4,500 built between their conception in 1957 and the end of building in the late 1980s.

TANK ENGINES

Industrial Tank Engines

Tank engines were first associated with railway building when contractors, employing huge groups of navvies, needed locomotives to replace the use of horses in moving heavy materials. The early tank locomotives were compact and economical, and light enough to work over poor tracks. Because the weight of the fuel and water bore directly on the driving wheels they were also able to negotiate tight curves and yet have sufficient adhesion to draw heavy train loads of earth and materials.

The contractors' tank engine quickly grew into the industrial steam locomotive as we know it today. They found a ready use in the emergent industries of the 19th century such as collieries, quarries, foundries, docks and harbours and other multifarious activities that became connected to the main line railway network, but required their own locomotives for the movement of materials and commodities.

The definitive industrial locomotive evolved with either side tanks or a saddle tank, and four or six driving wheels. Infinite variations were played on these basic concepts with engines superficially identical in appearance but having different cylinder sizes, wheel bases or even wheel arrangements. In the case of Britain, where industries were comparatively small, the typical industrial tank remained rela-

tively unchanged over more than a century's evolution. In Europe, Africa and America much larger examples evolved.

Main Line Tank Engines

The manoeuvrability of main line tank engines rendered the type suitable as standard forms of shunter on main line railways. The 0–6–0 was widely used as typified by the Midland Railway and LMS 'Jinties' and Russian 9Ps. Like their industrial counterparts, the main line shunter was built for over a century, the last one being the celebrated USATC 0–6–0Ts of World War II which saw service in many parts of the world and continued to be built in Yugoslavia until 1959.

Suburban Tank Engines

Tank designs were invariably chosen for the new suburban railways that had spread out from the ever-expanding conurbations as, again, the absence of a tender facilitated ease of running in either direction and saved the time-consuming business of turning. An obvious spawning ground for the first suburban tanks was London where the magnificent Metropolitan engines, fitted with

Below: A 0–6–0 tender tank, built in 1861, on the Belgium Teat Railway.

condensing apparatus, worked underground on the Metropolitan and District railways.

Busy suburban services around large cities were an early target for electrification and many displaced steam designs graduated to branch line and cross-country work. Interestingly, in their later years, some suburban engines gravitated to shunting yards whilst others passed into industry where they made strange bed-fellows alongside the typical 0–4–0 and 0–6–0 work horses.

Express Tank Engines

Express tanks were much more specialised and came in a number of magnificent forms like the 4–6–4 that appeared in both Britain and Ireland. The 4–4–4 accentuated the tank engine's symmetry to provide the ultimate in balanced proportions.

Express tank engines were patchy in their distribution. Russia, China, Africa and North America had little or no use for them, but in Europe they flowered as epitomised by the Prussian T14 class 4–6–4Ts. In the later years India took 2–6–4Ts and 2–8–4Ts, whilst Sumatra boasted a magnificent class of 2–8–4Ts built by Werkspoor of Amsterdam.

Tank+Tender Engines

Few tank+tender engines were built. Those that were, were essentially hybrids produced by their owners. The tenders, invariably locally built, were to provide extra fuel or water space. Such adaptations occurred particularly on plantation railways where small 'light' engines were running long distances over roughly maintained tracks.

Other instances involved transferring the water supply to a separate tender and removing the tanks from the locomotive. The two main reasons why this was done were that leaking tanks caused the driving wheels to slip, and low water levels in the tanks provided insufficient adhesion. In the latter case the removal of the tanks enabled steel waste and concrete to be placed in wheel splashers along the engine's running board for consistent adhesion.

Above: An Orenstein & Koppel 0–8–0 tender tank, built in the 1920s, in use on a plantation railway in Indonesia in the 1970s. This wood-burning locomotive represents one of many hundreds of such machines which were successfully used in industrial railways and plantations throughout the world.

Electric Multiple Units (EMU)

There is hardly a major city in the developed and developing world which does not employ some form of EMU to carry large numbers of passengers speedily within conurbations. The form has also been developed to include some of the fastest trains in the world, such as the French TGV and Eurostar.

The relative simplicity and reliability of electric motors and control gear at the turn of the century convinced far-sighted management that once the initial expenditure on fixed assets had been made, there would be subsequent savings in turn-round times, reductions in locomotive costs and staff, as well as cleanliness. All this would bring marketing and financial rewards.

An American, Frank Sprague, was the man who first made multiple unit operation practicable. Involving the control of two or more compatible units from a single driving position, his MU system was first used on the Chicago Elevated in 1897.

In 1905, the Metropolitan Railway (soon called the 'Metro', thereby coining the word for underground railways in general) joined the District Railway in London in converting its extensive network to 600V dc. This was also the voltage that was generally adopted by the surburban services of the London & South Western and South Eastern & Chatham railways which used the third rail current collection method.

Although underground and intensively worked surface lines followed suit all over the world, the EMU revolution was slower on the mainland of Europe, despite the fact that the Berlin U-Bahn and S-Bahn systems could be seen as good examples.

After World War II, Belgium and the Netherlands both introduced various types, the latter including some striking double-deck sets in 1994. Switzerland's Class 450 double-deck trains are interesting in that the power unit carries no passengers. Austria operates medium-distance expresses with multiple units, some of which once operated such trains as the 'Arlberg Express' from Zürich to

Above: This class 422, at London's Waterloo station, is of the type that works from the London terminal on the Southampton, Bournemouth and Weymouth expresses.

Below: An early LMS 3-car DMU is typical of the type that were prolifically used on the route connecting Oxford and Cambridge.

THE MULTIPLE UNIT REVOLUTION

Vienna. The CIS has many solidly built EMUs, and sets of Russian manufacture can be found, for example, on the Budapest Metro.

The Far East has its share, with modern metros in Hong Kong and the New Territories. Bombay's intensive local services have several modern EMU sets and, in Australia, many suburban services around Sydney are operated by modern double-deck units.

The British third rail network in the south has operated express EMUs since the 1930s including the prestigious 'Brighton Belle' Pullman train. Today, neat 5-car 'Wessex' express sets with a service speed of 110mph (177kph) link London to Weymouth. New, aluminium bodied, two and four-car 'Networkers' with a 75mph (120kph) service speed are spreading rapidly.

Diesel Multiple Units (DMU)

Diesel multiple units find favour where electrification is too expensive and where significant, fluctuating traffic makes the flexible operation of multiple-units economically sound. They are also found where modernisation is necessary to retain traffic on lightly used lines. In North America, the first commercial DMU was the single-car introduced by Budd in which motored passenger cars are added together to form the train.

The first British DMUs began cross-country services in 1954 and, from 1957, an important main line service from London to Hastings used 6-car express sets. They were discontinued in 1986 when the line was electrified.

With the demise of steam traction, the use of DMUs spread rapidly. However, the hope of retaining a share of the traffic from the onslaught of buses foundered on the closure of country stations. Today, a wide range of modern vehicles serve branch lines, outer suburban, cross-country and even the London–Exeter main line, where purpose-built 3-car diesel-hydraulic sets are to be found.

France and Germany also favour the DMU, with Germany having cross-country 2-car sets with a tilting mechanism based on the Italian, Fiat-built Pendolinos.

Below: One of the new Networker EMUs. These aluminium-bodied trains, introduced in 1991, are used for the services between London and Kent.

Diesel Locomotives

The compression-ignition system, invented by the Englishman Herbert Ackroyd Stuart, and developed between 1886 and 1890, laid the foundation of the engines that became known by the name of the Paris-born engineer Rudolph Diesel.

Transmission of the power to the wheel rim posed several problems that were approached in various ways. Today, mechanical transmission is usually confined to relatively low power units such as shunters (switchers), while hydraulic transmission is found in machines of higher power, especially those manufactured to German designs. Electricity is widely favoured to power the final drive of larger locomotives.

Although experimental units were developed in Germany and Britain, the first batch production was by GEC (USA) with three diesel-electric switchers in 1918. In October 1925, Alco delivered the first of a production series of 300hp diesel-electrics, the first of which ran until 1957. The first successful main-line locomotive was a 2,600hp diesel electric built by the Canadian Loco Company for Canadian National Railways in 1928. Powered by British Beardmore engines, it served until 1946.

Although no great progress was made with shunters until the late 1930s, in 1931 an 0–6–0 shunter, rebuilt from a steam locomotive using a Paxman engine with Haslem and Newton hydrostatic transmission, went into regular service in Britain. In 1935, yard diesels began to gain favour in the USA with Alco and GEC to the fore. It might be argued that the demise of steam on main line duties began in 1935, when the Baltimore & Ohio Railroad took delivery of an 1,800hp machine for use on passenger duties.

Adoption worldwide soon followed with hydraulic transmission for main line locomotives proving extremely successful in Germany and, to a lesser extent, in the United Kingdom where these designs closely followed German practice, Voith

Above: An impressive line-up of electric locomotives belonging to the Anshan (China) Mining Administration.

transmission being the system frequently preferred. Arguably, the most successful diesel-electric locomotives for high speed are the 'InterCity 125', 43xxx series. These haul the British 'High Speed Train', with a speed of 148.8mph (238.9kph) and they currently hold the world-speed record for diesel power.

Electric Locomotives

The first successful electric locomotive was made by Robert Davidson in 1842. Although this engine ran on the Edinburgh & Glasgow Railway and hauled about 6 tons at 4mph, it was not until 1879, when Werner von Siemens demonstrated a practical 4-wheel locomotive at the Berlin Exhibition, that engineers began to seriously consider the idea of electric traction.

Direct current supply and control is simple and was, indeed still is, often the preferred method for final drives. Since the first electric locomotives in regular service appeared on the City & South London Railway in 1890, the pace of development grew fast. In 1904, the Metropolitan Railway received its first batch of double-bogie locomotives which took dc current from a third rail. In rebuilt form, they served for many years and a working example still hauls special trains today.

Alternating current has many advantages including higher practical voltages, lighter overhead line equipment, opportunity for current regeneration and the absence of commutators. Brown-Boveri of Switzerland took the lead in ac electrification in 1899 when the 28-mile (45km) long Burgdorf–Thun Railway introduced 0–4–0 locomotives for freight traffic.

Electrification of the long Swiss tunnels was an obvious development. Ganz of Budapest and Brown-Boveri carried out the first high voltage ac electrification between 1902 and 1910, notably in the Simplon Tunnel where they employed a 3,000 volt, 15 cycle, 3-phase current on the overhead line equipment.

Only in recent years has it been possible to install and successfully control 3-phase ac traction motors, and a good example is the Swiss Class 460 with sophisticated electronic control equipment. All four axles on the 84 tonne machine are powered by fully suspended motors which provide an hourly rating of 6,100kW (8,177hp) and a service speed of 143mph (230kph).

Above: A Class 37 diesel electric on the North Wales, Crewe–Holyhead line approaching the end of its journey.

Left: The ETR450 Italian Pendelino tilting train was introduced on the Rome–Milan service in 1988. It was able to travel the 586 kilometres between the two cities at an average of 148 kph, including a stretch over the Po Plain at 200 kph. It completed the journey in just under four hours, a saving of over an hour from the previous best time.

Below: Built in 1931, this Paxman-engined 400hp diesel locomotive was one of a type fitted with hydraulic transmission.

3 *Great* BUILDERS

George and Robert Stephenson

The world's first locomotive works were set up in Newcastle upon Tyne by George and Robert Stephenson in 1823. After the construction of *Locomotion No. 1* in 1825, and *Rocket* in 1829, the works produced a stream of locomotives, including the 'Planet' type 2–2–0s and 'Patentee' 2–2–2s. By 1855 the Stephensons had completed over 1,000 engines, many exported to places as diverse as Australia, Egypt, Holland, India and Turkey, and, in 1882, China. By 1901, the business had become so successful that it was forced to move to a larger site at Darlington. In 1937 it took over R. & W. Hawthorn, Leslie & Co. Ltd. becoming Robert Stephenson & Hawthorns Ltd.

The Vulcan Foundry

In 1830 Charles Tayleur established a works at Newton-le-Willows in Lancashire. The first engine was built in 1833 and the company produced various locomotives for railways in Britain, Europe and the United States. In 1847 the company name was changed to the Vulcan Foundry Co. and in 1852 built its first locomotive for India, a 5ft 6in gauge 2–4–0 for the Great Indian Peninsula Railway. In the 1870s Vulcan also built Fairlie type articulated locomotives for use in New Zealand and Peru as well as *Taliesin* for the Festiniog Railway in 1876. By the end of the century, much of the company's work was destined for India, a trend that continued well after 1900.

Beyer Peacock

Beyer Peacock was founded in 1854, and a year later the first order for eight standard gauge 2–2–2s for the Great Western Railway had been completed. Although the company built locomotives for export, it also supplied considerable numbers of engines to British companies such as the Great Central, the London & South Western and the London & North Western railways.

Sharp Stewart

The Glasgow firm of Sharp Stewart began as the Manchester company Sharp Roberts, which had been established in 1828. Most early locomotives were 2–2–2s, many of which were exported to Europe. Roberts left the firm in 1843 after which it traded as Sharp Brothers. In 1852, when Charles Stewart joined the firm, it became Sharp, Stewart. By 1872 the company had outgrown the site at Manchester, and the operation was moved to Glasgow. In the 1890s the firm became famous for the engines it built for Britain's railways, including the famous Highland Railway 'Jones Goods' 4–6–0s.

Other British Companies

The Hunslet Engine Company was set up in Leeds in 1864 and the four- and six-coupled tank locomotives it built became the staple product of the firm, used by industry and railway contractors. The firm also built many narrow gauge engines for slate quarries and mines in North Wales. Another company famous for tank engines was the Glasgow firm of Neilson & Mitchell. Production started slowly, but by 1865 it had built over 760 locomotives. In 1900 it employed over 3,500 people and was one of the largest private locomotive building firms in the country. The Scottish firm of Andrew Barclay was also best known for the countless tank locomotives it built for industry from 1859 onwards. Dübs & Co. had been set up by Henry Dübs, who had managed Neilson's until the early 1860s. From 1867 the firm constructed engines for India, Cuba, Spain, Finland and Russia, as well as others for railways in China and New Zealand.

Railway Company Works

Since the first railways in Britain had no facilities to build locomotives of their own, they bought locomotives from the private companies previously described. Within a few years, railway companies began building their own works, which would enable them to construct and maintain their own fleets. Most of the works were built on a vast scale, employing thousands of staff, and new communities grew up around these great enterprises. By 1900 most of the major British railways had their own works, and had created 'railway towns' such as Crewe, Derby, Doncaster and Swindon where the social, economic and even political life of the area was influenced by the great workshops that dominated them.

Above: The Vulcan Foundary of Newton-le-Willows sold locomotives to many countries. Here we see a 4–6–0, destined for export, being loaded onto a ship.

AMERICA

was established in 1831 by Matthias Baldwin, a jeweller and well-known supporter of the abolition of slavery in America. The company he founded went on to become one of the most famous in the world. The fortunes of the Philadelphia company were, however, transformed by the arrival of Samuel Vauclain, who had served an apprenticeship on the Pennsylvania Railroad. An able administrator, businessman and locomotive designer, Vauclain rose from workshop foreman to president of the company. He experimented with compound locomotives, and in 1883 produced a 2–10–0 that had high and low pressure cylinders in parallel. Vauclain retired as company chairman in 1929, but was still president when he died in 1940. Such was the influence of the company that it has been calculated that ultimately the Baldwin company produced 1 in 11 of all engines built worldwide.

William Norris

Another company which was important in the 19th century was William Norris & Co. It was Norris who pioneered the use of the 4–4–0 wheel arrangement that became the standard in the United States until the 1890s when larger engines were constructed. Norris locomotives had bar frames and haystack boilers that were a development of four-coupled engines built by Bury for the Liverpool & Manchester Railway in Britain. Adding a leading bogie, Norris created a 4–2–0 which, although popular in the United States and abroad, was only a forerunner of the widely used 4–4–0 design. Norris was also responsible for the construction of the first 4–6–0, a freight locomotive built for the Chesapeake & Ohio Railroad and named *Thatcher Perkins*.

William Mason

Further innovations came from the Mason Machine Works at Taunton in Massachusetts. William Mason was responsible for the design of a number of what became known as Mason Bogies that were variations on the articulated Fairlie patented in Britain. Almost 150 locomotives of various types were built including, in 1881, three 2–4–6 engines for the New York & Manhattan Beach Railroad. Mason was also a pioneer of the idea of standardisation of component parts between locomotives.

Above: The Norris locomotive works, Philadelphia, first published in the *US Magazine* in 1855. In an age before electric lighting, note that, to provide enough light, the workbenches are placed under the many windows.

Below: Here men are engaged in the tedious work of hand-riveting the boiler cases at the Norris locomotive works in Philadelphia. As with the picture above, this scene was first published in the *US Magazine* in 1855.

AFTER THE OPENING of the first transcontinental railroad in 1869, the growth of the railway network in the United States was dramatic. With the increased size of the American railway system, by the turn of the century track mileage had increased to over 72,000 and with it came an increased need for locomotives and rolling stock.

Although locomotives were imported from Europe in the early days, an American railway industry grew up very quickly. By the 1850s a form of design suited to the operational requirements of US railroads was already beginning to emerge, which was much different to European practice. Features included robust construction, bar frames, 'haystack' fireboxes and large grates, which were necessary to counteract the poor coal available to some operators. Some railroads, like the Baltimore & Ohio, the Pennsylvania Railroad and the Southern Pacific, had their own workshops. However, some companies preferred to buy their locomotives from the firms that expanded as the railroad market did.

Matthias Baldwin

In the 20th century, the American scene was dominated by the 'Big Three' companies, Alco, Baldwin and Lima, but before 1900 there were many smaller firms who produced locomotives. In the early years the most prominent firms were those of Baldwin, Norris and Rogers & Cooke. The Baldwin company

H. K. Porter

H. K. Porter was another of the smaller manufacturers in the USA, one of a number who built mainly industrial type engines. Even in 1947, an advertisement for the Pittsburgh company showed lightweight 2–6–2 and 2–8–2 tank locomotives built for sugar plantations in South America, looking very similar to the locomotives built by them half a century before.

Left: A work's plate of the Pittsburg, PA, locomotive building firm of Henry Porter. Porter's first locomotive was built in 1867, their final production being out-shopped in 1951.

Above: This picture of Baldwin's erecting shop, which was first published by *The American Railway* in 1892, shows that in almost 40 years since the Norris pictures (opposite) very little had changed. At this point the concept of assembly-line production was still some years off.

19TH CENTURY EUROPEAN BUILDERS

France

As a reaction to the uncontrolled growth of railways in other countries during the 'railway mania' period, railway development in France was affected by government controls. The country was divided into geographical regions, and strict limits were placed on companies operating routes within these areas. Although this avoided the proliferation of lines seen elsewhere, it could also be argued that it stunted the growth of railway development. Since it was English engineers, such as Joseph Locke, who had helped build the first main lines, it was English locomotives, like the Allan 2–2–2s later nicknamed 'Buddicoms', which were used in the early years of French railways. English influence continued with the introduction of locomotives designed by Thomas Crampton, over 320 of which were used extensively on the Northern and Eastern railways. Locomotive building continued in centres such as

Fives-Lille and Decauville, but it was not until the last two decades of the century that French locomotive design became prominent with the activities of Alfred de Glehn at the Société Alsacienne's factories at Mulhouse and Belfort. De Glehn's pioneering work with compounding began in 1885. His first locomotive was for the Nord company, and such was the influence of his ideas, and the work of rivals such as Henry of the PLM, that by 1902 the seven major French railways had 1,128 compound engines. By this time too, the 4–4–0 wheel arrangement had become common in France, and was not superseded by larger designs until after the Great War.

Germany

Although, as we have seen, the first engine to run in Germany had been a Stephenson 'Patentee',

Above: One of Russia's many locomotive factories at St Petersburg. This picture, from the 1890s, shows the entire work force.

Below: This handsome 4–2–0 Crampton-type locomotive was built in 1852 by the French firm of J. F. Cail.

48

Left: **The Henschel engineering works at Kassel, Germany, in 1837. On the right of the picture is the dome of the old steam house. This is the site where, in 1848, the firm was to produce their first locomotive, *Drache* ('Dragon').**

Der Adler, by 1863 only 15 per cent of the locomotives running in that country were imported. The most important manufacturers were Borsig, Henschel and Maffei. August Borsig originally set up a factory in Berlin-Moabit in 1841. His early engines were built for the Berlin to Anholt line and the Cologne–Minden route, the first, *Borsig No. 1*, being closely modelled on the American 'Norris' type. By 1846, a total of 120 engines had been built, and the company went on to be one of the biggest builders in Europe. The other two firms, Henschel of Kassel, and Maffei of Munich, also grew from small beginnings into large companies, whose products were exported far beyond the German border. Maffei, in its earliest days had built Crampton locomotives for the Baden State Railways and, in 1890, was responsible for building what was then the largest

locomotive in Europe – an 0–6–0+0–6–0 Mallet semi-articulated for the Gotthard Railway in Switzerland. In 1896 they built a number of the pioneering 'Victor Emanuelle' 4–6–0s for the Upper Italy Railroad company. The Chemnitz firm of Richard Hartmann was also active in the period, building many articulated locomotives after 1910.

Austria, Romania and Czechoslovakia

Austria had embraced railways almost as enthusiastically as the German states, and so it was not surprising that railway builders grew up there too. The dominating figure during this period was that of Karl Gölsdorf who, in 1891, became the Chief

Mechanical Engineer of the Austrian State Railways. The railway had works at both Vienna and Floridsdorf where Gölsdorf designed mainly compound engines for running trains over the steeply graded lines of the Austrian Alps.

The firm of Ganz of Budapest were extremely important innovators in the production of electric locomotives in the period leading up to the end of the 19th century. Their chief engineer, Kando, was ahead of the rest when he produced a 500V 3-phase locomotive as early as 1896. It was tested on a line in Budapest three years later. In the 1920s the Pilzen firm of Skoda began to construct locomotives, mainly to existing designs, for the new Czechoslovakian railway system.

49

Above: A worm's-eye-view of new locomotive wheels at China's Datong locomotive works.

Britain

In 1903 the largest locomotive firm in Europe was created when the three Glasgow firms of Dübs, Neilson Reid and Sharp Stewart were amalgamated to form the North British Locomotive Company. By World War I they had built over 5,000 locomotives both for home and export. Between 1920 and 1940, the company's export business was balanced by a healthy trade at home, with locomotives being built for all the 'Big Four' railway companies. Unfortunately in 1962, the company was forced out of business by competition from abroad, particularly the USA, and it went into liquidation.

USA

A similar consolidation of companies had also taken place in the USA by the creation of the American Locomotive Company (ALCO). By 1910 this amalgamation of ten companies had created one of the legendary names of locomotive building in America. From its plant at Schenectady the company built many locomotives for American railroads. One of their famous designs was the F15 class Pacifics for the Chesapeake & Ohio Railroad, which became the prototype for many similar engines in later years, such as the Northern Pacific 4–8–4, which was built from 1926 onwards. Perhaps the ultimate in American locomotive power was the 4–8–8–4 'Big Boy' of which 25 were built for the Union Pacific Railroad. Further changes occurred in 1916 with the take over of the Lima Works. The employment of a new designer, William E. Woodard, began a process that would make the company truly one of America's 'Big Three' manufacturers. The company began building 'super-power' engines in 1925 with the construction of the 'Berkshire' class 2–8–4s for the Boston & Albany Railroad. Even larger engines were built, culminating in the construction of 2–6–6–0 Mallet designs for the Chesapeake & Ohio Railroad. The construction of the 'Big Boys' may well have been the zenith of steam construction in America for, from the 1930s, new firms grew to build the fast growing phenomenon of diesel and electric traction. In 1930 General Motors acquired the Electromotive and Winton companies, and with these on board it began working to perfect diesel technology. The standardisation policy it began in 1937 with the 'E' series diesels had far reaching effects on the industry. By the 1970s General Electric was the only real competition for GM, with famous names such as ALCO, Baldwin, Lima and Fairbanks-Morse having left the locomotive building business.

Europe

In Europe in the 1930s other new firms began to build new rolling stock, with car manufacturers such as Michelin and Bugatti in France beginning to make inroads into the diesel and electric train market.

In post-revolution Russia the pace of locomotive building slowed and it wasn not until the 1930s that there was a reorganisation of locomotive building. Although steam was its main work, the Kolomna Works turned out its first diesel in 1930. The Lugansk Voroshilovgrad Works were enlarged in the 1930s to build larger 2–10–2 locomotives, but during the Second World War the whole operation was relocated to Krasnoyarsk. After the war, all Russian works built steam locomotives, but in 1950 work was concentrated at Voroshilovgrad and Kolomna with steam production ending in 1956.

China

Much attention has been placed on the works at Datong, but two other centres warrant a mention. At Tangshan, in Hebei Province, a thriving works existed, building locomotives for home and export use until 8 July 1976, when an earthquake struck the city, killing 148,000, including 6,000 employees of the works. Despite this disaster the city and the works have been rebuilt, and by 1986 annual production was back to 80 locomotives. Another important works was at Dalian on the South Manchurian Railway. Manchuria was occupied by the Japanese during the 1930s in which time the company constructed 'Liberation' 2–8–2s, a type that had originally been built by ALCO during World War I, thereby introducing a distinctive American influence into Chinese locomotive design.

Below left: The ornate, and typical early 20th century doorway over the head offices of the North British Locomotive Company in Glasgow.

Below: A British Railways standard Class 9, 2–10–0, fitted with a Franco-Crosti boiler, under construction at Crewe Works in 1955.

ALTHOUGH THE RAILWAY builders of the modern era, like their Victorian counterparts, build locomotives and rolling stock for railways worldwide, gone are the famous names such as North British, Lima, Alco, Baldwin and Beyer Peacock. These firms are now mostly replaced by new names that are often part of multi-national companies, of which railway manufacturing is only one area of their business.

The General Electric Company

The English Electric Company was a famous name in England, building diesel and electric locomotives for use in Britain and abroad. Perhaps best known for its influence on the design of the widely used 08 class diesel shunters used on British Railways, the company was taken over by GEC in 1971. The General Electric Co. was active in the USA during the birth of both diesel and electric traction, and is now an enormous undertaking, with interests far beyond the sphere of railways. The British part of the corporation was itself the subject of a merger, becoming GEC Alsthom in 1989. The new organisation employs over 16,000 people with factories in Britain and France. In 1989 it supplied electrical equipment for the Class 91 InterCity 225 trains that are used on the newly electrified East Coast Main Line.

Brush Traction

This is another British firm that has been working closely with the former British Rail and the newly privatised companies. Remembered by many diesel enthusiasts as one of the builders of the long-lived Class 47 diesel locomotives, more recently they have built Channel Tunnel *Le Shuttle* locomotives for Eurotunnel, and the new Class 92 engines.

General Motors

Another huge company, it has its international headquarters at La Grange, Illinois. Through licensing agreements with, among others, Hyundai in Korea, Clyde Engineering in Australia, and the Turkish State Railways, GM is prolific and builds locomotives all over the globe. The arrival of GM Class 59 locomotives in Britain in 1986 for use on

Foster Yeoman stone trains marked a new era in British locomotive operation. Another big order is that from the newly privatised English, Welsh & Scottish company, which ordered 250 Class 66 locomotives.

Europe

German firms are also important in the manufacturing scene. Adtranz was formed through the merger of ABB and AEG and although having its headquarters in Berlin, has factories in Austria, Denmark and Finland as well as Crewe and Derby in England. Adtranz won a contract in 1996 to build new stock for Chiltern Trains, the first British order for some considerable time. The firm was also heavily involved in construction of locomotives for Eurotunnel. The Munich firm of Krauss Maffei are an old firm with great experience in the manufacture of electric locomotives, and continue to do so, manufacturing stock for Germany, Spain, Iran and Turkey most recently.

Elsewhere in Europe, Fiat have pioneered the use of heavy road diesel engines for railway use, and build electric and diesel locomotives, particularly for Italian Railways. Two other established companies continue to build for their own railways: Ganz Hunslet of Budapest for Hungarian State railways, and Skoda, at Pilzen, for the Czech and Slovak railways.

China and Russia

The Chinese locomotive works at Datong achieved fame as the last railway works producing steam locomotives for general use. Opened in 1959, Datong has over 8,000 staff, and although production of steam locomotives has now ceased, it still manufactures passenger and freight locomotives, shunters and component parts such as bogies. China also has another works at Qishuyan in the Jiangsu Province, which builds diesel electric locomotives of the 'Dong-Feng' type.

In the Russian Federation, the Kolomna Works in Moscow, is still in existence, building diesel electric engines of the TEP70 type. There are also works at Kaluga, where Lyudinovo build diesel-hydraulic and diesel-electric locomotives, mainly for industry. There is also another significant operation at Michurinsk in the Tambou region.

Above: **Building the Class 465 at Metro Camel works, Washwood, Birmingham, England.**

Left: **Building** Le Shuttle **at Brush, Falcon works in Loughborough, England.**

4 *great* RAILWAY Journeys

ARGUABLY THE MOST FAMOUS of all express trains is the 'Flying Scotsman'. Although the name itself was not brought officially into use until after the creation of the LNER in 1923, the name had long referred to the train that left King's Cross at 10am each weekday bound for Edinburgh. Running over the lines of three companies – the Great Northern, the North Eastern and North British railways – the 393-mile (632km) journey was hardly rapid, taking 9 hours in 1876.

Until the 1930s, handicapped by a restrictive agreement between the East and West Coast companies, who limited the London to Edinburgh services to 8 hours, the journey remained slow. In 1928, the train achieved the longest non-stop run in the world with Gresley A1 class Pacifics fitted with corridor tenders to allow locomotive crews to change en route. In May 1932, 25 minutes was cut from the timetable and, by the outbreak of World War II, the journey time was down to 7 hours and 20 minutes. New luxurious rolling stock was also introduced, with innovations such as a cocktail bar and hairdressing salon as well as restaurant cars. It was on this line, just north of Peterborough, on the 15-mile (24km) long Stoke Bank, that in July 1838, Gresley's A4 class streamlined Pacific, *Mallard*, obtained the world steam speed record of 126 mph.

After World War II, journey times were steadily reduced so that when, in 1978, 'High Speed Trains' were introduced, the trip took only 4 hours 52 minutes. On the electrified East Coast route today, this prestigious service now takes the unprecedented time of 4 hours 12 minutes.

The 'Cornish Riviera Limited'

When the London to Penzance line opened in August 1859, not only did almost all the trains stop at all stations, but passengers also had to change at Exeter and Plymouth. On arrival in Truro a horse-drawn bus took them on to Falmouth, where the travellers boarded the West Cornwall standard gauge line for the 33 minute ride to Penzance. The fastest journey took some 14 hours 50 minutes.

The 'Cornish Riviera Limited' ('limited' in that originally only a certain number of places on the train were available) evokes images both of seaside holidays in Devon and Cornwall, and the speed and quality of GWR services between the two world wars. The train originated with the inauguration of the 'Cornishman' express, which in 1890 was not only the fastest train between Paddington and the West Country, but also one of the fastest on Britain's railways, being able to reach Penzance in 8 hours and 42 minutes. After the conversion from broad to standard gauge, in 1892, the 'Flying Dutchman' cut a further 15 minutes off its time and so became the fastest train in the world. Although never officially used in GWR publicity material, the name pioneered the running of non-stop trains to the West Country, and was adopted when the 'Cornish Riviera Limited' was begun in 1904. The combination of more powerful locomotives and the use of 'slip' coaches, that were detached at intermediate stations en route without stopping, the 'Limited' became the Great Western's premier express. Leaving Paddington at 10.30 in the morning the train, in the summer of 1939, reached Penzance in 4 hours 2 minutes, taking slightly longer in winter.

One of the highlights of the journey is the 1,110ft- (338m) long Royal Albert Bridge, which spans the River Tamar separating Devon and Cornwall. Widely regarded as Brunel's masterpiece, its unique design is a combination of enormous cast iron trusses and chain link suspension bridge. It took seven years to build and was opened by Prince Albert in May 1859.

Below: The up 'Flying Scotsman' enters Newcastle Station. Hauled by an A4 Class Pacific, this scene of the early 1950s shows the train en route to London's King's Cross Station.

Right: A CPR transcontinental passenger train pauses on a horse shoe-shaped wooden trestle a few miles west of Schreiber, Ontario. This temporary trestle was one of the first to be replaced by an embankment.

THE CANADIAN PACIFIC transcontinental railway took ten years to build, the last spike being ceremoniously driven in at Craigellachie BC on 7 November 1885. Taking three days and three nights, the 2,915-mile (4,700km) journey from Montreal to Vancouver has the distinction of being the longest possible journey in North America which passengers can take all on one train.

After travelling through Quebec and into Ontario, the train runs along the shores of Lake Superior. After crossing hundreds of miles of pre-Cambrian shield to Sioux Lookout, it then winds its way through the Manitoba Lake District to Winnipeg, which it reaches late on the evening of the second day. After an hour's stop the train is usually made up to 18 cars, including two baggage vans, eight sleepers, one super-dome observation car and two restaurant cars, all hauled by three locomotives. The train then continues west across the rolling prairies to Saskatoon, Saskatchewan, and Calgary.

Edmonton, Alberta, which it reaches on the afternoon of the third day.

After Edmonton begins the climb to Jasper, high in the Rocky Mountains. From here the train carries on through the mountains, going over Yellow Head Pass and down to Kamloops. The final part of the journey is beside the Fraser River down to Vancouver. Passengers are well looked after with excellent meals, sleeping cars and showers. On a historical footnote, it was on this line, in 1954, that the first streamlined sleeper train, 'The Canadian', was introduced by Canadian Pacific.

Juliaca to Cuzco, Peru

The 211-mile (339km) long Peruvian Central Railway is the highest in the world and is regarded as one of the wonders of railway engineering. It crosses the deep Rimac Valley between Lima and La Oroya, and climbs nearly 13,000ft (4,000m) within a distance of less than 47 miles (75km), although the twists and turns which the railway needs to gain height make the journey 73 miles (117km). To gain height and at the same time keep the gradient down to the necessary 1 in 23 the line uses the whole width of the valley, crossing frequently from one side to the other. Between Chosica and Ticlio, the highest point of the line at 15,693ft (4,783m), there are six double and one single zigzags, 66 tunnels (including that at Galera which is 3,860ft (1,176m) long) and 59 bridges (including that over the Verrugas, which, when it was built in 1890, at 575ft (175m) long, was the third longest in the world).

Operating the line is beset with problems. Not least of which are the lack of local sources of fuel; heavy wear and tear of locomotives and rolling stock; and frequent landslides and washouts. Steam power is still the preferred method as diesel units are prone to losing power in the rare air and as such often have difficulty in taking the gradients. Although the Central Railway was built for carrying ore from the La Oroya copper mine, the incredible journey is still available to travellers, even if they have to be given oxygen by the train attendants.

From Calgary the train follows the Bow River and enters The Gap. This is a tedious upward climb, winding among the crags and crawling along terraces to the summit at Stephen at an altitude of 5,329ft (1,624m). This is the Divide, where the water from the glaciers split to run down either side of the mountain. From here the train descends alongside Kicking Horse River. Such is the gradient on the descent, that the train has to go through many spiral tunnels that take it on its way to

Above: In Canada winters can be, and often are, very severe. Here we see a diesel-hauled train receiving minor attention before it continues on its journey.

THE SOUTH AFRICAN 'BLUE TRAIN'

Above: Interior view of the luxurious South African 'Blue Train'.

THE FIRST LUXURY TRAIN to run from Cape Town to Pretoria was started in 1903. In 1910, on the formation of the Union of South Africa, the train was named the 'Union Limited'. Always associated with travel of the highest standard, the twice-weekly train was renamed the 'Blue Train' ('Bloutrein') in April 1939. While the locomotives continued to be in the black of South African Railways, this change of name coincided with the introduction of new blue and cream carriages with clerestory roofs.

First class tickets for this train were severely limited. Those fortunate passengers who are able to pay the supplement are cosseted in an air-conditioned, dust-proofed paradise with super de luxe blue leather upholstered seats, loose cushions and writing tables with headed note paper.

Such was the popularity of the train that, in spite of the high prices, reservations had to be made long in advance. To provide room for the various on-board services, including a bathroom, only 100 passengers could be catered for on each journey. The train was electrically hauled by blue locomotives between Pretoria and Kimberly and again between Beaufort West and Cape Town and scheduled to do three round trips weekly from October to March and one from April to September.

President Nelson Mandela inaugurated the 'new' 'Blue Train' in June 1997. Built on the frames and bogies of the original 'Blue Train' sets, these two new trains feature two grades of on-board accommodation – luxury and de luxe. The luxury suites differ from the de luxe in that they are more spacious and offer larger bathrooms – deluxe with private shower or bath, luxury suites have baths. All the suites have televisions and telephones, while the luxury suites in addition have CD players and video recorders. There is also a 24-hour butler service, laundry service and two lounge cars, as well as a camera positioned in the front of the train, which gives passengers a 'driver's eye' view of their 999-mile (1600km) long, 26-hour journey.

Lagos To Kanu

After leaving Lagos the first part of the 925-mile (1,488km) long journey follows the Ogun river valley before the line climbs steadily to the university city of Ibadan, 800ft (244m) above sea level. If the journey is taken a few weeks into the rainy season the forests on either side of the line abound in vivid

greens and most of the stations have brilliant flamboyant trees under which the local people do their domestic work and children play. Near Offa the line enters the less fertile and open country of the north and descends to the Niger at Jebba, some 500ft (152m) above sea level and 302 miles (486km) from Lagos.

The line first reached Jebba in August 1909 and in October of that year a steam train ferry, *Fabius*, entered service. On New Year's Day 1912, through

Left: The new South African 'Blue Train', en route to Cape Town between De Dooms and Worchester, is seen here being hauled by three Class 5 E-1 electric locomotives.

communication between Lagos and Kano was established when the Jebba–Minna (460 miles – 740km – from Lagos) section of the line was opened. The ferry was only a temporary arrangement and by 1910 the 659ft (200m) long North Channel bridge, with two 105ft (32m) half-through spans and three 30ft (9m) concrete arches, was completed. The South Channel, however, was more difficult to bridge. The 1,523ft (464m) long bridge consisted of seven 183ft (56m) spans with three 30ft concrete arches at each end, was eventually opened on 31 January 1916.

After crossing the bridge, from which there is a fine view of the memorial to the explorer Mungo Park, the train runs north-east towards Zungeru and Minna from where it commences its long climb to Kaduna (1,961ft – 600m). It is after here that the highest point on the line, Zaria, some 2,200ft (670m) in altitude and 620 miles (1,000km) from Lagos, is reached.

THE 'ORIENT EXPRESS'

EUROPE'S BEST KNOWN train is the 'Orient Express'. It was founded by Georges Nagelmackers, a Belgian mining engineer, who, in 1876 ran his first through train, complete with sleeping cars, from Paris to Vienna. By 1883, with the completion of a line through Turkey, it became possible to make the journey from Paris to Istanbul entirely by rail. The 1,857-mile (3,000km) journey took 77 hours, crossed six countries and used ten railway companies. In 1888, the train changed its route, by diverting at Budapest and going by way of Belgrade, Nis, Sofia and over the newly opened line to Plovdiv. Passengers were able to enjoy the comfortable sleeping cars with velvet curtains, plush seating and the tinkling hand-bell in the corridors that summoned them to five-course French *haute cuisine* in the dining cars.

Named the 'Orient Express' in 1891, it made cursory frontier stops to change engines. The clientele always included government couriers, chained to their diplomatic bags, and often royalty and diplomats also used the train.

After the opening of the Simplon Tunnel in 1906, a rival service was inaugurated. The new service, which was called the 'Direct Orient Express', ran from the Gare de Lyon station in Paris, by way of Switzerland, Austria, Italy and what was later Yugoslavia. Both trains were suspended during the two world wars, but in the inter-war period they typified luxury train travel. The service was never the cheapest with the operators, the International Sleeping Car Company, charging considerable supplements over normal first class fares, making the trip the province of the wealthy and famous.

The train was the scene of much intrigue and mystery, both fact and fiction, and was immortalised in Agatha Christie's famous novel *Murder on the Orient Express*. It was also on the stretch of the line that runs along the Aegean coast to Thessalonika, that Ian Fleming's *From Russia with Love* was filmed.

The service was withdrawn in 1977, but in more recent years has been re-introduced by a new company VSOE ('Venice–Simplon Orient Express') who, using restored rolling stock, have recreated the glory days of this great express.

The 'Dogu Express'

If desired, the traveller can carry on from Istanbul and take the 1,208-mile (1,944km) railway journey to Kars, the last town in Turkey before the Armenian frontier. From Istanbul the railway runs along the north coast of the Marmora Sea before crossing the Ak Ova Plain. After ascending 965ft (294m) through a narrow gorge, whose walls are 300ft (91m) above the railway, the train reaches Bilecik, a steam-lovers' paradise where Turkey's last huge steam banking 2-10-2 tank engines hauled trains the ten miles up another 1,280ft (390m) at 1 in 40, to Eskesehir on the Central plateau. From Eskesehir a branch line turns east to Ankara, formerly called Angora, but renamed in 1921 by Attaturk when he made it his nation's capital. After reaching Ankara, at an altitude of 2,875ft (876m) feet, the line continues for 186 miles (300km)across the plateau before dropping 1,000ft (305m) at Pazali. From Sivas the Dogu continues at approximately the same level, turning south-east and climbing over the foothills to reach the Upper Euphrates valley at Cetinkaya.

The next section, the 31 miles (50km) to Erzincan through the narrow Atma Gorge includes 13 tunnels and is a masterpiece of Turkish engineering. In between the tunnels every kind of bridge – stone, underslung girder, concrete and box girder – is found crossing over the clefts and tributaries that run into the Euphrates gorge. After Erzincan the line turns north and climbs to about 1¾ miles (3km) into the long Horasan Tunnel. The final part of the journey is the 1 in 40 descent of the fir-covered hills to Sarikamis. Kars is not too far away and the trip from Europe into Asia is over.

Above: The Train Captain makes final checks before the Orient Express departs.

Left: Passengers dine in five-star luxury on the Orient Express.

THE TRANS-SIBERIAN RAILWAY

ALTHOUGH NINE DAYS on a train might not be everybody's idea of fun, a journey on the 'Trans-Siberian Express', to those who have not made it, sounds the most exciting and romantic journey in the world. The huge distances involved in the construction and operation of the railway are difficult to comprehend. Almost 6,000 miles (10,000km) in length it is the longest railway in the world, linking Moscow in the West to Vladivostok in the East. Although, as early as 1858, proposals were first made for a railway that would connect Moscow to the Pacific, it was not until 1875 that an official plan was put forward.

Construction started in 1891, but the line was not completed until 1904. Despite having to disembark from their trains at Irkutsck, to cross Lake Baikal by ferry before completing the rest of their journey, passengers began to use the service, since it cut many weeks from the journey from the Far East to Europe. In the winter, the ice on the lake, the deepest in the world, became so thick that the train was run over rails specially laid over the lake. The line round the southern shore of the lake was not built until 1905. Such was the terrain of this 42-mile (67.5) section that no less than 38 tunnels had to be bored. In places the shore of the lake is almost vertical and up to 4,000 feet high.

At first, because of the comparatively flat land of Manchuria part of the route was laid across Chinese soil, thereby making the line both cheaper and shorter. However, after the Russo–Japanese War, a connection was built from Chita via the Amar Valley and Khabarovsk. Although considerably longer than the direct route across Manchuria, it did ensure that the whole route was over Russian territory.

One of the most interesting features of the line is the number of bridges, the crossing of which is a most emotive sight. On the western portion of the line alone, there are eight bridges of over 1,000ft (300m) in length. These include those over the Irtish (six main spans and 2,100ft (640m) long), Ob (seven main spans and 2,670ft (814m) long), and Yenisei (six main spans and 2,800ft (853m) long). At Khabarovsk, on the North Manchurian frontier there is another exceptionally long bridge across the River Amur.

In 1913, an English traveller wrote a detailed account of his journey in which he described his train, headed by a highly polished Pacific locomotive, as being composed of long green and gold carriages. He also related how the corridors were carpeted and that the dining car was decorated with an ivory-white ceiling, large plate-glass windows and panelling.

It was said that it was the British who named the service the 'Trans-Siberian Express'. There were two weekly trains. One of which had Wagons Lits rolling stock and a coach equipped with a travelling bathroom, a gymnasium, a chemist's shop, a lounge complete with piano and reading and games rooms. All were, no doubt, necessary on a trip that might last three weeks, at an average speed of less than 25mph (40kph). In the inter-war years, Westerners were forbidden to travel hard class and their spacious and clean compartments were only polluted by a loudspeaker that exuded the sort of thing expected from Stalinist Russia.

The journey is rather more comfortable today. Although the line is now fully electrified, there are 91 stops between Moscow and Vladivostok, a city only recently accessible to the Westerner since the break up of the Soviet Union. Tea is always on tap from coach samovars which is brought to compartments by the attendants. The best time to traverse Siberia is autumn when the monotonous landscape of birch trees turn to the colour of burnished gold.

Right: The Trans-Siberian Express pauses at one of its stops during its journey across the former Soviet Union. Taken in the mid-1980s, a few years earlier such a picture would have resulted in the photographer's immediate arrest for espionage.

5 Shaped for SPEED

SINGLE WHEELERS AND INSIDE CYLINDER 4–4–0S

Singles

The express locomotive with a single pair of driving wheels, which developed from *Rocket* and the 'Planet' type on the Liverpool & Manchester Railway, led to both the inside cylinder 'Jenny Lind' type 2–2–2 designed by E. B. Wilson of Leeds, and the Sharp, Stewart 2–2–2, many of which were built for railways around the world. As Britain was at the forefront of railway engineering technology, having workshops and foundries to construct locomotives, these British-built or designed 2–2–2s were some of the first locomotives used on the railways in Germany, Holland and France.

Outside Cylinder Types

After the 'Jenny Lind' and Sharp's 2–2–2s, the next design, of any distinction, was the 'Crewe' or 'Buddicom' outside cylinder 2–2–2 for the LNWR. This type was also copied and used on a number of European railways, notably in France, where William Buddicom set up a foundry that built some of that country's first locomotives. By 1860, the 2–2–2 had evolved into the 4–2–2, the most famous of which was Gooch's GWR broad gauge 'Iron Duke' type single used on the main line expresses out of Paddington to Wales and the West of England.

By 1870, Patrick Stirling, of the Great Northern Railway, had designed his famous locomotive with eight foot diameter driving wheels. Samuel Johnson of the Midland Railway, had also built his 'Spinner' type 4–2–2s which headed most of the important passenger trains on that railway. The LNWR had followed on from the 'Crewe' type with a number of classes of single-driver express locomotive. These included the famous 'Lady of the Lake' 2–2–2s and *Cornwall*, a one-off example by Francis Trevithick which, due to its long service, had to be rebuilt three times during its working career. The Caledonian Railway built a one-off example in the form of locomotive No. 123 that was used in the 'Race to the North'.

By the 1900s, the 2–2–2 and other single types were no longer in vogue, although the GNR, under Henry Ivatt, built a small batch of 4–2–2s to replace the Stirling singles which had been withdrawn. The design was obsolete and largely out of use by the 1920s.

Inside Cylinder 4–4–0s

From the late 1880s most British railways were running 4–4–0s. The Great Western had the famous 'City' class including *City of Truro*, which won its place in history when, in 1904, with an 'Ocean Mail Special' from Plymouth to London, it allegedly topped 103mph over the Devon banks, the first recorded case of a locomotive exceeding 100mph. These sturdy machines continued until the late 1940s when the last batch of 4–4–0s, the VS class, was built for the Great Northern Railway of Ireland.

The Midland Railway successfully constructed a large number of compound type 4–4–0s which were in traffic from the 1900s until the late 1950s. The Caledonian Railway, in Scotland, constructed large groups of 4–4–0 tender locomotives, the most famous of which were the 'Dunalastair' class which survived in traffic until 1961. The LSWR, under Dugald Drummond, also built sizeable numbers of 4–4–0s of various classes to tackle the many varying types of traffic on the system. The best known of these was the Class T9, which, after rebuilding by Robert Urie, saw many years of traffic, the last not being withdrawn until 1961.

Across the Channel the French PLM had 'Wind Cutter' compound 4–4–0s and Austria and Germany their Gölsdorf compound 4–4–0s. It was, however, the USA that built more 4–4–0s than anywhere else in the world. Many of these were for export to South America and even to Russia and Australia, the final examples being built in the 1920s. In Europe, the 4–4–0 type had an even longer life with the final examples not going until the early 1960s while in South America they lasted until the 1970s.

Below: One of Patrick Stirling's fabulous Singles approaches Quorn, Leicestershire, on England's Great Central Railway.

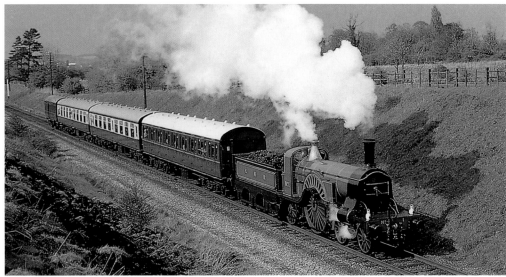

ATLANTICS AND TEN-COUPLED ENGINES

Below: A GNR large-boilered locomotive at Harringay, London, in the early 1920s. A point of interest is the somersault semaphor signal arm on the left of the picture.

Bottom: The Prussian State Railway was a user of Atlantics. Their power, generated from the large firebox, makes this type excellent, both for heavy trains at medium speeds and sustained fast running with moderately loaded trains.

The Atlantic in Britain

The Atlantic 4–4–2 type was a direct follow-on to the 4–4–0 type. Most railways of the world had this type of locomotive and many examples were built. In Britain the Great Northern Railway had both large and small boilered examples, designed by Henry Ivatt. These machines were used on all the crack expresses on that system from the 1900s until after being 'cascaded' down to secondary work. The last examples were withdrawn in the early 1950s. The Lancashire & Yorkshire Railway also used Atlantic type locomotives, designed by J. A. F. Aspinall. These locomotives were in express passenger service well into the 1920s when the last examples were withdrawn. John G. Robinson, of the Great Central, designed some very fine Atlantic locomotives for the opening of the London Extension to Marylebone in 1899. These locomotives, nicknamed 'Jersey Lillies' were in express passenger use until the late 1940s.

Although the Great Western did not make great use of this wheel arrangement, George Jackson Churchward had at least two Atlantic locomotives constructed at Swindon as an experiment. These were later rebuilt as 'Star' class 4–6–0s. He also ordered three French-built De Glehn compound Atlantics for comparison and they were later rebuilt with Swindon boilers, lasting in traffic until the 1920s.

The Atlantic in North America

From the 1890s through to the 1920s, the Atlantic type was used extensively on most Grade A main line railways in North America, especially on the east coast. Some of the type were built as 'Camel-backs', so called because the cab was mounted in the centre of the boiler above the driving wheels, giving the appearance of a camel's hump. The last North American Atlantics were withdrawn in the late 1950s, when the Pennsylvania and the Reading railroads retired their last examples, which had been used on suburban work.

The Atlantic in Africa

The 4–4–2 design even appeared on the Egyptian State Railway network where at least 30 lasted until the late 1950s. The last known use of Atlantics anywhere in Africa was a class of Henschel-built examples belonging to the Caminhos de Ferro de Moçambique (Mozambique State Railways) which were in everyday use as late as 1975.

Ten-Coupled

The 2–10–0 heavy freight locomotive had its origin around 1900, when several railways throughout the world, especially in North America, developed this type of locomotive for heavy haulage use. In Europe the 0–10–0 and 2–10–0 were developed, especially in Germany and Austria, for similar purposes. The most famous German types were the Class 44 and Class 50/52UK 2–10–0s, which were built in large numbers both before and after World War II. The Prussian State Railways and the Deutsche Reichsbahn also had 2–10–2Ts that were used for freight and banking duties. As well as building for the domestic market, large numbers of German 2–10–0s and 2–10–2Ts were also built for the Turkish State Railways. The Austro-Hungarian Empire had large groups of 0–10–0s and a number of 2–10–0s built to the design of Karl Gölsdorf, some of which were exported to Greece and Yugoslavia.

In Britain there were only two main classes of 2–10–0, both developed by R. A. Riddles. His first design, an austerity type 2–10–0 for the War Department which, like their 2–8–0 sister locomotives, were shipped to Europe in large numbers after D-Day. Riddles' other design was the successful BR Standard 9F 2–10–0, of which many were built after 1954. The last main line steam locomotive built in the UK, *Evening Star*, was a 9F, and was out-shopped from Swindon Works in March 1960.

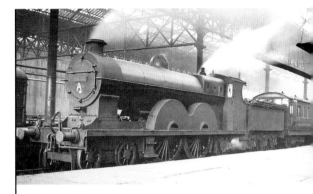

Above: One of Aspinall's Lancashire & Yorkshire Railway Atlantics, with 7ft 3in (2210mm) driving wheels. Forty of these impressive locomotives, called 'Highfliers', were built between 1889 and 1902 for working fast passenger services.

Right: A China Railway's Japanese-built Class SL7 Pacific. This magnificent locomotive from the streamlined era of the 1930s was one which used to work the 'Asia' high-speed express between the important industrial cities of Dalian and Shenyang, or Mukden as it was then known.

Below: One of the Chicago Milwaukee, St Paul & Pacific Railroad's Hiawatha trains. Introduced in 1935, they were the fastest scheduled steam trains ever to run.

IN EUROPE AND NORTH AMERICA, the streamline or Art Deco Era started in the late 1920s and early 1930s. By the mid-1930s a distinct style of design and artistic direction had been reached which covered all aspects of life in an age of moulded metal and Bakerlite.

Britain

In Britain, as elsewhere, the movement had a profound effect on transport. One of the best examples is the LNER 'Silver Jubilee' train of 1935 that had some of the most advanced carriages in use on any British railway of the period. Not only were they ahead of their time in construction terms, but they also incorporated amenities and features that were almost unheard of in everyday use at the time. These included an internal telephone system between carriage compartments and the dinning car to order meals, and an early form of air conditioning. Another example is the LMS 'Coronation Scot' of 1938 which incorporated many of the features of the 'Silver Jubilee'. Unlike the former train, however, it used modified existing Stanier-designed carriage stock and had 'Princess Coronation' Pacific locomotives fitted with curvaceous streamlined casing.

Germany

During the 1930s, in Germany, the Deutsche Reichsbahn built its own streamlined trains. These were largely constructed for propaganda purposes, especially in conjunction with the 1936 Berlin Olympic Games. These trains gave the impression of great advancement in railway technology and speed to the foreigners who attended the games, or visited the country as tourists. In truth, however, the streamlined 03 class Pacifics and Class 05 4–6–4s were no faster, or more efficient, than their non-streamlined counterparts. The carriage stock, however, was of a more advanced nature, and incorporated mechanical improvements to that used on conventional trains. These trains continued in regular service until the outbreak of war in September 1939.

In 1932, in addition to the steam-hauled streamliners, the Germans built the famous two and three car diesel express trains known as the 'Flying Hamburger' units. These were used on a number of express schedules from some of the larger cities and were still in use in the former East Germany until the early 1960s.

USA

As an image boosting policy, most Grade A railroads built streamlined express locomotives and stock. An example was the Milwaukee Railroad's 'Hiawatha' train. At first it was hauled by 4–4–4 types. The train was, however, so popular that its weight demanded a more powerful locomotive and a 4–6–4 had to be developed. On the New York Central, the 'Drefus' streamlined Hudsons on the '20th Century Limited' were, due to their speed and efficiency, ahead of their time. The Norfolk & Western arguably built the most beautiful of all America's streamlined locomotives – the J Class 4–6–4. These fine locomotives headed all the N&W's most important trains from the 1940s until the 1950s. On the Southern Pacific the 'Daylight' 4–6–4s, painted in their orange, black and silver livery, blazed the trail to the Far West. They paved the way towards the first streamlined diesels – the E and F classes that finally brought the steam streamlined era to a close in the early 1950s.

The Far East

In Japanese occupied China (Manchuria) the Japanese started experimenting with a streamlined train called the 'Asia Limited'. In the last years of the 1930s, this train ran at 80mph (129kph), along well-maintained track. This was the first step that would eventually lead to the electric 'Bullet' trains of post–war Japan.

The locomotives and rolling stock of the Art Deco era lasted in many cases into the 1950s and 1960s, well after the era of Jellymold and Bakelite had past into memory. To this day, the legend of that age still continues to inspire and fascinate artistically minded people everywhere.

Below: A streamlined LNER locomotive built at Doncaster, England, between 1935 and 1938. The best known of these A4 Class engines is No. 4468, 'Mallard', which set a speed record of 126 mph (203 kph) in 1938.

"THE CORONATION"
ON THE EAST COAST ENTERING SCOTLAND
IT'S QUICKER BY RAIL
FULL INFORMATION FROM ANY L·N·E·R OFFICE OR AGENCY

DIESEL STREAMLINERS

Above: A dual-mode diesel-electric FL9 built by EMD for the New Haven Railroad, now operated by Amtrak.

Right: A modern Midland Mainline Class 43, ready to depart from London's St Pancras station.

THE PERIOD BETWEEN the two world wars saw the increasing use of diesel traction for longer distance passenger services. This was a time when, not only were engineers becoming more interested in aerodynamics in their search for higher speed for the same power, but also when 'marketing people' were seeing the public appeal of sleek and fast trains.

Europe

Germany and France were early in the field with the USA not far behind. In 1933, Germany produced the two-car articulated diesel set that ran between Berlin and Hamburg called the 'Flying Hamburger'. It is said to have been the test bed for U-boat engines and is credited with achieving 108mph (175kph). The following year, in France, the Nord system introduced a three-car diesel electric set that ran between Paris and Lille.

USA

However, it was in the USA where diesel traction found most favour and streamliners proliferated. The Burlington's 'Pioneer Zephyr' captured the imagination with a three-car set powered by General Motors' engines with ribbed stainless steel bodywork that became the hallmark of the Budd Corporation. On 26 May 1934, this train covered the 1,015 miles (1,633km) between Chicago and Denver in 13 hours 5 minutes at an average start to stop speed of 77.6mph (124.9kph). The Union Pacific also entered the field in 1934 with an unusual looking three-car set, the bulbous nose having a prominent air intake grill. One set, M 10001, operated the 2,272-mile (2,656km) 'City of Portland'

service between Chicago and Portland on a 39-hour schedule. When heavier trains were required to cope with the demand generated by these services, for all practical purposes, the power units themselves became locomotives. 'Skirts' were installed between bogie sets and flexible fairings between coaches reduced drag while the end vehicle, often an observation car, was rounded into a 'beaver tail' bringing the curving profile almost to rail level. Individual main line diesel locomotives adopted streamlined forms but it is doubtful whether there was any practical benefit as speeds were not likely to be sufficiently high to make the smooth contours aerodynamically effective.

Post-War Development

Trans–European expresses, including 87mph (140kph) double-ended diesel hydraulic sets of German origin, were introduced in 1957. In 1959, Britain was slightly faster with the 90mph (145kph) 'Bristol Pullman' and 'Sheffield Pullman' sets which also had power-cars at each end. In 1969, Britain was at the forefront of high-speed streamliners when she experimented with the Advanced Passenger Train. This four-car articulated unit, powered by gas turbines, had a tilt capability which allowed substantial speed increases on conventional track. Much important technical information was obtained which was used in the development of an electric APT which, on 10 August 1975, achieved a speed of 152mph (245kph). This had a power car in the centre of the set which obviated the need for a high voltage bus-bar throughout the train. Experience gained from both the gas turbine and electric APTs, which Britain failed to exploit, laid the foundation for the several tilting electric express trains of today. Doubts about the viability of the APT spurred the production of a fleet of high-speed diesel-electric sets that became probably the best units of their kind in the world, the 'InterCity 125s'. The trains can be varied in length and composition by the provision of a power car at each end of rakes of Mk III coaches. Various engines up to 2,700 horsepower enable the sets to operate at a service speed of 125mph (200kph), although they can achieve much higher speeds. Similar sets were also built in Australia where they are called XPTs.

ELECTRIC STREAMLINERS

THE STREAMLINING OF HIGH SPEED electric trains followed naturally upon the marketing success of diesel powered streamliners in the late 1930s to mid-'50s. Electric traction meant that trains could run regularly at speeds of over 100mph (160kph). Aerodynamics could then make a genuine contribution to the efficiency of the units by giving a higher speed for the same power, or a heavier train with the same service speed.

Britain

Like the majority of diesel trains, the electrics usually have power units at or near each end with non-powered passenger coaches in between. The 25kV development of the Advanced Passenger Train described in the previous section, underwent extensive testing on BR and provided the basis for development by other countries but it did not enter revenue service and was retired to the Railway Age museum at Crewe. Although very few electric locomotive-hauled trains qualify for streamline status in Britain, a Class 91 on a rake of Mk IV coaches might be an example.

Sweden and Italy

Sweden and Italy have both produced successful streamlined tilting sets. Development of the Swedish X2000 began in the 1970s, with the first of 20 sets going into service on 5 September 1990. Running between Stockholm and Gothenburg, they cut the journey time for the 285 miles (459km) from 4 hours to 3 hours 11 minutes. Their immediate success led to interest in other countries, including the USA where a set was tested in Amtrak livery. Italy also started to work on tilt trains in the 1970s, launching the first series production streamlined ETR 450 (Eletrro Trenni Rapidi – soon nicknamed 'Pendolino') in 1987/88. Many of the coaches are motored thus spreading the weight of equipment and reducing axle loads. Unlike some other streamliners, where the end cars are power units only, passengers are carried in all vehicles. These sets were so successful that successors, the ETR 460s, were soon ordered.

France and Switzerland

Switzerland realised that such trains were a potential answer to the rapidly increasing costs of providing new infrastructure. A consortium of the Italian and Swiss state railways and the Bern–Loetschberg–Simplon, Cisalpino AG, has nine sets operating from Milan over the three main arteries in Switzerland to Geneva, Basle and Zurich.

France saw the solution to high speed travel in a mix of modified and purpose-built sections with trains using proven technology. Thus was born the TGV ('Train à Grande Vitesse') series which, with modifications, include the multi-current 'Thalys' sets which are ultimately planned to operate international services through France, Belgium, the Netherlands and Germany. The Channel Tunnel Eurostar sets owe much to the TGV concept. Production TGV's have power cars at each end and first entered service in 1981. The familiar wedge shape can be seen widely, not only in France, but also in Switzerland. A double-deck 186mph (300kph) version is under development.

Germany's similar approach to France introduced ICE 401 sets with neatly rounded streamlining. Test speeds exceeded 248mph (400kph). They are extensively used throughout Germany and can be seen on through services in Switzerland.

Japan

The majority of streamliners use conventional technology, either on modified or specially built lines. The Japanese Shinkansen (new trunk line) not only led the way, but was revolutionary in that it is self-contained and traffic is confined to passengers. The Tokyo–Osaka line opened in 1964 with 12-car sets, each end of which have a prominent coned appearance. The sight of these illuminated at night earned them the name 'Bullet trains'.

Left: One of France's Train à Grande Vitesse (TGV) Atlantiques travelling at speed (they can reach 300 kph) through the French countryside.

Below: The 'Thunersee' ICE (InterCity Express) arrives at Interlaken West in Switzerland almost at the end of its journey from Berlin. Power cars of Class 401 at each end have a maximum rating of 6400 hp and a maximum service speed of 280 kph.

6 Built *for* Heavy HAULAGE

THE CONSTRUCTION OF *Royal George* for the Stockton & Darlington Railway marked a new beginning in locomotive development. *Royal George* was the first 0–6–0 mixed traffic locomotive to be built and heralded the start of an entirely new group of locomotives that would, in the early 20th century, evolve into the heavy freight locomotive. During the Victorian period there were two main types of locomotive, namely passenger and freight. In the early days passenger locomotives were normally 0–4–2 or 2–4–0 wheel arrangement, while the goods, or baggage locomotives as they were originally called, were mostly 0–6–0 tender or tank engines.

By the 1880s, the majority of railway companies, both in Britain and in Europe, were building larger 0–6–0 goods engines and experimenting with the first 0–8–0 heavy freight locomotives. In America, where there were longer trains, the locomotive manufacturers were designing and building larger and heavier 2–6–0 and 2–8–0 locomotives for heavy freight haulage. These bar-framed locomotives were well suited to the rough terrain and track of the pioneer American railroads and were also exported in large numbers to South America, Australia and New Zealand.

With the turn of the 19th century a large number of railways in Europe and North America were looking for designs to cope with the ever-increasing tonnage of freight. It was realised that the existing designs would not satisfy the demand for the longer, heavier trains that were needed. In Europe, this led to the production of heavy 0–8–0, 0–10–0 and 2–10–0 locomotives for heavy freight and switching duties.

Austria and Germany

In Germany and Austria, various standard classes of locomotives evolved for this purpose. Karl Gölsdorf in Austria perfected several classes of successful 2–8–0 and 2–10–0 heavy freight locomotives that were not only used within the Austro–Hungarian Empire, but also exported in numbers to other countries in Europe. One country in particular which imported Gölsdorf locomotives was Greece, where the State Railways operated a large fleet of 2–8–0s and 2–10–0s.

The Prussian State Railways of Germany designed a number of standard classes of heavy freight locomotive based on common parts. These included the Class G8 0–8–0, Class G10 0–10–0 and Class 44 2–10–0 that were in minor production when the German railways were amalgamated into the Deutsche Reichsbahn in 1922. These standard designs were also exported in large numbers to other European railways including Rumania, Poland, Bulgaria and Turkey.

Russia

The development of railways in Russia, from the 1830s, necessitated the import of foreign designs, mainly British and German, to evaluate a satisfactory formula for future home-built types. Later, factories using capital raised at home and from abroad, were set up to develop locomotives of suitable designs and these were often based on British, German or American practice.

The need to construct large numbers of standard passenger and freight locomotives, with the ever increasing length and weight of trains, heralded the production of the O class standard 0–8–0s. This Tsarist period design, with only minor modifications, continued to be manufactured by Russian locomotive workshops into the first two decades of the 20th century. However, in the years leading up to the 1917 October Revolution the various private and state owned railways in Russia were already taking delivery of large batches of German and American designed 0–8–0s, 0–10–0s and, shortly before World War I, 2–10–0s.

By the 1920s, the Soviet Government had designed and manufactured several standard classes of locomotive for heavy freight use. These included the E class 0–10–0s, the FD class 2–8–2s and the American-built Baldwin and Alco 2–10–0s supplied to Russia during World War I.

Below: **A typically British inside cylinder 0–6–0 as exported to the East Indian Railway under the BESA standard designs at the beginning of the 20th century. This particular locomotive, a work's shunter at Luckow, was built by the Vulcan Foundry in Lancashire in 1909.**

BANKERS AND HUMPERS

TOWARDS THE END of the 19th century, with the ever-increasing weight and length of passenger and freight trains, it became apparent to most large railway organisations that there was a need to develop classes of banking, or 'helper', locomotives to ease heavy trains over mountainous terrain. For many decades the larger railway companies had been using conventional 4–4–0 and 0–6–0 locomotives for this purpose which, to a greater or lesser degree, had been successful. However, by the late 1880s it was becoming apparent that the problems that emerged from the use of heavier trains could not be satisfied by using existing locomotives.

North America

One of the first railroads in North America to address the problem was the Baltimore & Ohio which, in 1904, constructed the first Mallet locomotive to be used in the USA. This locomotive, nicknamed *Old Maud*, was used experimentally to bank heavy trains over long, tortuous inclined sections of track that had previously required the use of multiple-heading of locomotives. In the years following the construction of *Old Maud*, most of the larger railroads in North America built, or ordered, similar Mallet or conventional 2–8–0 or 2–10–0 type locomotives to bank, or help, trains over heavy inclines.

Britain

The Midland Railway constructed an 0–10–0 tender locomotive which also had nicknames. It was sometimes called *Big Emma* and at other times *Big Bertha*. This locomotive, built in 1919, was used on the Lickey Incline at Bromsgrove, near Birmingham where it successfully operated on banking duties until 1956, in which year it was withdrawn and replaced by a BR Standard 9F class 2–10–0.

On the Great Central Railway, John G. Robinson designed some 0–8–4 tanks for heavy hump shunting in goods yards. These machines lasted in traffic until the late 1940s, surviving long enough to be taken into BR stock. In 1925, the LNER ordered a Beyer Garratt locomotive, for use on the Worsborough Incline near Barnsley. This 2–8–8–2 wheel arrangement machine survived in traffic until the line was electrified in 1955, after which it was tried on the Lickey Incline in company with *Big Bertha* and was withdrawn for scrap in 1956.

In 1921, the London & South Western Railway ordered three 4–8–0 tank locomotives designed by Robert Urie. These machines were used at the newly-opened marshalling yard at Feltham to hump-shunt freight wagons into formation. All three were withdrawn in 1962.

India

In the early 1900s the British-administered railways of India also faced similar problems to those encountered in North America. The need to bank trains over heavy inclines necessitated the design and con-

Below: **The Midland Railway's unique three-cylinder 0–10–0 banking engine, which was built in 1919 for banking trains up the notorious 1 in 37 Lickey Incline on the Birmingham to Bristol main line. The engine spent its entire working life on this duty being allocated to Bromsgrove shed until its withdrawal from service in 1956 and subsequent breaking up at Derby Works.**

struction of a class of heavy tank locomotive built to the 0–8–4T wheel arrangement. These locomotives, along with some 2–8–4Ts, were used on the Ghat Incline of the Great Indian Peninsula Railway.

South Africa

South African Railways were quick to realise the value of heavy banking locomotives. Shortly before World War I, they ordered a batch of Mallets from North British of Glasgow. These machines were used on heavy freight and banking duties until the early 1950s, when they were withdrawn.

New Zealand

New Zealand Railways were also faced with the problem of how to move large passenger and freight trains over difficult terrain. However, looking at the matter from a different angle, they constructed an incline railway using the Fell system of braking which required the construction of specially designed 0–4–2 tank locomotives. The Fell braking system worked from a centre rail that retarded the locomotive and train whilst working on heavily graded lines. This often meant the use of several locomotives working together, depending on the weight of the train being banked.

Above: A former Great Indian Peninsular Railway Ghat Banker, in the form of Y4+0–8–4–T, in the sidings at Hindalco in Renukut.

Left: The world's last heavy duty 0–8–4 banking engine enjoys a further lease of active life at the Hindalco aluminium plant in Renukut. Having originally been built by the North British of Glasgow in 1920 for banking trains up the Ghats from Bombay on the Great Indian Peninsular Railway, this unique veteran was sold to Hindlaco from Parel works, Bombay, in 1970.

GARRATTS AND BIG BOYS

BY THE BEGINNING of the 20th century, the development of the heavy freight locomotive had reached an advanced stage. Quite apart from the conventional use of 0–6–0s, 0–8–0s and 2–8–0s, many main line railway companies were looking at alternative methods to overcome their operating problems.

Britain

In the years up to 1914, the majority of British main line companies had ordered or constructed some 2–8–0 freight locomotives. These included the Great Western that had a sizeable fleet of 2800 class 2–8–0s and nine 4700 Class large-wheeled 2–8–0s. The Great Northern Railway, under Nigel Gresley, designed some successful standard 2–8–0s for heavy coal and freight traffic from the North East to London. Perhaps the best known British heavy freight locomotive of the Edwardian era was the Robinson ROD (Railway Operating Division) type 2–8–0, many of which were constructed for use by the Army in World War I.

Classes P1 and 8F

After the formation of the LNER in 1923, Nigel Gresley designed two 2–8–2 Mikado type tender locomotives of Class P1 for heavy freight work from London, on the Great Northern main line. These locomotives were, if anything, too successful as they were so powerful that they would break the couplings of the small four-wheeled coal and goods wagons then in use.

The most successful heavy freight locomotive ever designed in Great Britain was Sir William Stanier's 8F class, built for the LMS from 1937 to 1944. These powerful 2–8–0 engines were so successful that the War Department ordered many batches. Many of these workded around the world, especially in the Middle East and Persia (Iran), where they were used to supply the Russians across the northern border.

The Garratt

In the British colonies the problem of operating heavy freight was overcome by conventional and articulated locomotives. In particular, the develop-ment of the Beyer Garratt locomotive after 1907 proved to be a remedy to some of the worst problems met by railway engineers and administrators. In South Africa the Class GL and GMAM Garratts were outstanding and successfully overcame many of the problems that had previously hampered railway operation.

Europe

By the 1880s the main line companies in eastern and western Europe were developing and building larger locomotives for mixed traffic as well as heavy freight. The Germans in particular saw the potential at an early stage for the use of such machines. Shortly after the formation of the Deutsche Reichs-bahn in 1922, construction of standard classes based on Prussian designs, was extended to include large numbers of 2–8–0s, 2–10–0s and 2–10–2Ts. In France the railway companies had benefited greatly from locomotive construction during World War I with the importation of 140C class 2–8–0s and American-built 'Pershing' type 2–8–0s. After World War II, the SNCF further benefited with the acquisition of 141R type 2–8–2s as part of the Marshal Aid Plan.

North America

By the early part of the 20th century the Americans had developed a sizeable network of railways operating express freight. The acquisition of mod-ern, efficient heavy freight locomotives to haul these trains was of paramount importance. A num-ber of larger railroads developed locomotives to meet this need. The Union Pacific in particular pro-duced two classes of locomotives of outstanding design. These were the 'Challenger' and the 'Big Boy'. Both types were developed from the late 1930s and construction continued until the late 1940s. They were to be the last heavy freight loco-motives in service on the Union Pacific and were not withdrawn until 1959. In a similar vein, the Norfolk & Western Railroad, which operated heavy coal trains in Virginia, had a large fleet of Y6B and A class Mallet articulated locomotives that gave outstanding service from the early 1930s. These machines were finally withdrawn in 1960 and were the last heavy freight steam locomotives in use in the USA.

Left: A former Rhodesian Railways 14A Class 2–6–2+2–6–2 Garratt pauses for refreshment at Balla Balla on its way from West Nicholson to Bulawayo. These splendid locomotives were exported to Rhodesia from Beyer Peacock's Dorton Manchester Works in 1953 and 1954.

Below: American steam super-power scaled down to metre gauge operation as one of the world's last Texas type 2–10–4s highballs across the metals of the Teresa Cristina Railway in southern Brazil with a rake of coal empties. These giants were built by Baldwin's of Philadelphia in 1940.

BIG DIESEL HAULERS

Above: **A Class 60 diesel electric hauls an aggregate train past Milepost 92½, near the Leicestershire village of Newton Harcourt, England.**

THE FIRST USE OF MAIN line diesels in North America was on the Rock Island Railroad in 1928. The seemingly rock-solid predominance of the steam locomotive and the private locomotive builders in the USA and elsewhere would, in a short time, be challenged and over a 40-year period be wiped out by this new form of motive power. The first major adoption of diesel units on the main line in quantity took place in the mid to late 1930s, when General Motors and General Electric started to market and mass-produce suitable power units. Initially, the main line railroads in the USA were very sceptical about this new form of technology. However, by the middle of World War II, most of the companies were convinced that this was indeed the future of railroad motive power.

The E and F Classes

By the mid-1950s, the diesel invasion had really taken effect in North America. Whole classes of near-new steam locomotives, some only eight years old, were laid-up and scrapped. They were replaced by the new standard E and F class units, the former for express passenger work and the latter for mixed traffic work. For switching purposes and trip working the manufacturers produced a whole series of Bo–Bo and Co–Co single-cab hood types. With such motive power on the market, sold at reasonable terms, most railroads found it very desirable to dieselise as soon as they could. The American manufacturers also sold their products on a worldwide basis – to South America, Africa, Asia, Australia and New Zealand. Some European countries, such as Spain and Portugal, also bought American diesels.

Gas Turbine Traction

The Union Pacific Railroad decided to try an experiment with gas turbine traction in the mid-1960s. This was successfully achieved with a fleet of gas turbine units that were used primarily for heavy freight work on the UP main line which were in operation until the late 1970s.

Britain

Diesels first appeared on the main line in Britain in the mid-1930s when the Great Western acquired a fleet of streamlined diesel railcars and parcel vans. These, together with some later additions built in the 1940s, lasted in traffic until the early 1960s. At the same time the LMS also ordered diesels. At first just shunting locomotives, but later they constructed a three-car diesel multiple unit and, in 1947, ordered two main line locomotives – No.s 10000 and 10001.

Also in 1947, the Southern Railway ordered three main line diesel locomotives that were not delivered until after the formation of British Railways in 1948. These three locomotives were to be the forerunners of the Class 40 main line locomotives of the 1960s. As a result of these early experimental

diesels, BR were able to implement the 1955 Modernisation Plan that led to the elimination of British main line steam in 1968.

Germany and Russia

The development of diesel traction in Germany started in 1932 with the introduction of the famous, streamlined 'Flying Hamburger' three-car diesel units, which later led to the construction of several experimental main line locomotives, both before and during World War II. The eventual outcome of this was the construction, during the

post-war years, of a modern locomotive fleet made up of diesel hydraulic and electric locomotives which replaced steam from the late 1950s onwards. The Russian State Railway benefited greatly from Lend Lease. After the war, large numbers of American diesel units were shipped to Russia. As a result of this translocation the Russian State Railway decided in the 1950s to construct their own modified versions of American technology. However, the Russian designs were not as good as the US counterparts and it was not until the 1980s, when outside technology was more available, that modern, efficient designs were made available.

Left: Chicago's La Salle Station and downtown skyline provide the background for a Rock Island E–7 642 with its cargo of commuters. The red and yellow paint scheme worn by the 642 was, at that time, the new image of the Rock Island.

Below: A multiple header hauling coiled steel to West Pittsburg, California. It is seen here traversing the famous Tehachapi Loop on the Sante Fe Railway.

IN THE EARLY YEARS 'Big' was consistent with size and weight. Modern technology, however, has led to lightweight locomotives with power outputs greatly in excess of the giants of yesteryear. Before the working of locomotives in multiple was developed, increasingly heavy trains called for more traction motors in one machine. This increased the length and weight, which not only had to be distributed over several axles, but also had to be flexible enough to negotiate curves.

Europe

The locomotives of the 'Frontier Railway', from Lulea to Riksgransen in Sweden, provide a good example. Iron ore is mined near Kiruna, 1,670 feet above sea level. Rail is the easiest way to get the ore to the coast at Narvik, Norway, from where it is exported. In 1914 ASEA/Siemens delivered 1–C+C–1 1,800 horsepower locomotives. In 1960 the line was using a Class DM3, a 1-D+D+D-1 giant of 270 tons rated at 9,750 hp with an overall length of 82ft 4in (25m).

In Switzerland and Austria, the celebrated 'Crocodile' electric locomotives were developed for the grades and curves of the region's mountainous lines. These 1–C+C–1 locomotives were so called because the centre cab windows ('eyes') and the sloping machinery compartment ('jaws') suggested that reptile. Switzerland also produced a variety of experimental multi-axle locomotives for the Gotthard route including a 236-ton 1–A+A–1–A+A–1+1–A+A–1–A+A–1, no less than 111ft 6in (34m) long.

North America

The first main line electrification in North America was on the Baltimore & Ohio between Camden and Waverley which introduced 1,440hp machines weighing 96 tons and capable of handling 1,870-ton trains. The Pennsylvania Railroad, the largest electric operator among the Class 1 roads, used the world renowned sleek and powerful dual voltage Class GG1, which ran passenger services between New York and Washington DC. The 2–Co+Co–2 machines weighed 230 tons, were 79ft 6in (24m) long and had a continuous rating of 4,260hp.

The Virginia Railroad introduced 30 'Triplex' locomotives, 1–B–B–1+1–B–B–1+1–B–B–1, 152ft (46m) long and capable of handling 6,000 short ton trains on 1 in 50 grades between Mullens and Roanoke.

Asia and Africa

Japan had some powerful Bo–Bo+Bo–Bo 120-ton machines on the Tokaido line but the palm for the 3ft 6in gauge goes to South Africa where three Class 3E 1,200 horsepower units in multiple lifted 1,500-ton trains from 2,210ft (674m) to 4,980ft (1,518m) on the Pietermarizburg–Glencoe line. Development was such that by the 1980s three Class 9E 5,070hp locomotives built by GEC of England, working in multiple, were handling 20,000-ton coal trains on 1 in 250 grades.

The 200 miles (322km) of electrified routes out of Bombay included the fearsome grades of the Ghats to Igatpuri. In 1925, 120-ton C+C locomotives producing 2,100hp and 2–Co–1 and 2–Co–2 passenger machines with a tractive effort of 33,600 pounds, were delivered. However, in 1951, Co+Co machines weighing 123 tons and with a tractive effort of 75,000 pounds began to supplant them.

The Asiatic Commonwealth of Independent States, part of the former USSR, has the largest locomotive on the continent. This Class WL 86, double Bo+Bo+Bo, 147ft 6in (45m) long and weighing 300 tons, can be seen on the Baikal to Amur line. Built at Novocherkassk in 1985/6 it develops 15,287 horsepower, has an axle load of 25 tonnes and is capable of 100mph (161kph).

Current practice

Switzerland has led the way in the effective use of modern technology and continues to do so today. The Class 465 Bo–Bo weighs only 82 tonnes and has a one hour rating of nearly 9,400hp. In July 1996, two similar Class 460s and two Class 465s positioned in a 3,212-ton freight train, lifted it over the 1 in 37 gradients of the Loetschberg at speeds on the climb ranging from 31 to 43½mph (50 to 70kph).

Right: **Britain's Class 92, built by Brush Traction at Loughborough, is fitted with TVM430 cab signalling for freight services through the Channel Tunnel. It has a maximum speed of 140 kph.**

7 Diesel *and* Electric TRACTION

THE ADVENT OF DIESEL POWER was not greeted with quite the same enthusiasm as had been evident with the introduction of steam locomotives, but this may have been because the early diesels were crude and under-powered in comparison with those of today. The principle of the internal combustion engine had been established as early as 1794, but it was not until 1883 that Daimler patented the high speed petrol engine, closely followed by Rudolf Diesel's 'oil engine' in 1892. Two years, later the first locomotive to use this new form of motive power was built by Priestman Brothers of Hull, who completed a 12hp dockyard shunter with an 'oil engine' and mechanical transmission. In 1896, another diesel engined locomotive was constructed for use in Woolwich Arsenal in London. This 9hp, single-cylinder machine was built by the Grantham firm of Hornsby & Son, and proved successful, although rather under-powered. They were useful enough, however, to persuade the War Office to order a further four, the last being delivered in 1904.

Diesel Railcars

It was not until 1912 that the next major breakthrough was made, with the construction of the world's first diesel powered railcar. Built by the Sodermanland Midland Railway of Sweden, the railcar was an adapted coach, fitted with a diesel engine and generator. Further examples were made for other Swedish railways by Allmänna Svensa Aktiebolaget. In the same year, Rudolf Diesel experimented with the construction of a diesel locomotive, but its direct transmission was not a success.

The First World War restricted the development of diesel motive power, and it was not until the 1920s that significant progress was made, although petrol-engined railcars had been produced in the USA during this period. In 1917, the General Electric Company built a railcar with electric transmission for the Delaware & Hudson Railroad and it was not long before there was quite a number at work on lines in rural America. The first really successful diesel locomotive was a 300hp shunter constructed in 1924 by Alco, General Electric and Ingersoll Rand for the Jersey Central Lines. A further 26 similar locomotives were produced in the next two years for various railways and industrial concerns. One of the designers of this engine was Alphonse Lipets, a Russian émigré who had worked on a highly experimental diesel locomotive built by the Soviet Railways in 1924.

Streamlined Diesels

It was not until the 1930s that diesel power began to really become a major force in railway development. Important improvements in diesel technology, including a reduction of the weight of locomotives, and increasing the power of drive units, made diesels more attractive to railways. Much of this new technology was used in the streamlined express trains such as the Burlington Railroad's 'Pioneer Zephyr', introduced in 1934. The Union Pacific Railroad inaugurated its own streamlined diesel services in the same year. Some idea of the impact of the new 1,200hp locomotives was that the M10001 cut the 2,272-mile (3,655km) journey from Chicago to Portland by 18 hours in October 1934.

Other railways all over the world built and operated similar trains. The famous 'Flying Hamburger', built for the Deutsche Reichsbahn, was a glamorous propaganda tool for Nazi Germany, and there were similar streamlined units used on Austrian and French railways before World War II.

In Britain, the 'Big Four' railway companies were still unconvinced of the merits of diesel power for high-speed main line travel, and experimented with less powerful railcars for use on secondary or branch lines. The GWR introduced a new diesel railcar in 1934, developed in conjunction with the bus manufacturer AEC. Successful, both in traffic and as a publicity exercise, the company ordered a further 17, before building another 20 to their own design at Swindon, the last being completed in 1942.

Above: A Baltimore & Ohio EMC 'EA' No. 51. This was the first streamlined diesel electric not part of an articulated set. The shell is now preserved at the B&O Museum in Baltimore, Maryland.

Below: An early LMS diesel electric 0–6–0 shunting locomotive, as introduced on that railway during the 1930s. The LMS received engines from both Armstrong Whitworth and English Electric. Diesels were first employed on shunting duties, on which they offered many advantages over steam. The early LMS diesel shunters of the 1930s were the immediate forebears of the later 12000 Class, which formed the basis for today's standard 08 design.

DIESEL REPLACES STEAM

USA

It was in the United States that the race to replace steam with diesel began in earnest. The General Motors company began this process in 1937, when they built the first E1 type 1,800hp passenger locomotive. This engine was significant since it was the first of a standardised design. Customers could choose single cab or cabless power units, setting a trend in US railroading, where operators could mix and match power units where appropriate. Within two years, a more powerful 2,000hp version, the E6, was built, and this was followed in 1939 by a freight version, the FT.

During the following decade, the rate at which dieselisation took place in the USA was breathtaking. In 1938 there were only 314 diesels at work on American railroads, but by 1950 this total had risen to nearly 12,000.

The Road Switcher

In the post-war era, 'road switcher' or 'hood' type of locomotive was developed. This had a full–width cab with the rest of the engine contained within a narrow hood with external walkways on either side. These locomotives were much uglier than their predecessors, but soon became a familiar part of the railway scene in the USA. Well over 10,500 of Electro-motive's GP road switcher engines of various types were sold to US railroads, from 1949 to 1975. The early 1,500hp GP7 was superseded by ever more powerful variations, so that by the middle of the 1960s, power ratings of 3,600hp could be achieved.

The 'Centennial' Class

In 1969, the world's largest and most powerful single unit diesel the 'Centennial' class was built for the Union Pacific Railroad. Constructed by General Motors their name celebrated the 100th anniversary of the driving of the Last Spike of the transcontinental railroad, the 47 locomotives in the class had huge 6,600hp engines. Most railroads were happy with lower ratings that could be bolstered by additional 'slave' units that could be coupled to the main locomotive according to the load being moved. By the 1960s only two main manufacturers dominated the scene in the United States, General Motors and General Electric. Firms such as Alco, Baldwin, Fairbanks–Morse and Lima, so dominant in the age of steam, had faded from the scene.

Europe

In Scandinavia and Europe, the introduction of diesel traction took many different forms, and did not occur in quite the same dramatic way it had done in the United States. Some, although not all, countries used the expertise of American companies, such as General Motors, to build and equip their railways with diesel locomotives. This was the case in Sweden, although by the 1960s the 8,386-mile (13,493km) long State Railway system was run by diesel and electric locomotives almost equally. General Motors' equipment has also been used in Denmark where, as recently as 1981, 3,240hp ME class engines were ordered by the Danish State Railways for passenger and goods traffic. In Spain, locomotives from another American company, Alco, were also purchased. Elsewhere in Europe the situation was much more varied. In France and Italy, railways built their own diesels, with the most individual nation being Germany. After World War II, German manufacturers and the Deutsche Bundesbahn moved almost entirely to the adoption of diesel-hydraulic locomotives. It was generally thought that high-speed engines with hydraulic transmission through cardan shafts would produce both powerful and reliable locomotives. In 1953, five prototypes were constructed by Krauss–Maffei for the Deutsche Bundesbahn, each locomotive having two 1,100hp Maybach engines. After successful trials another 100, of what were to become known as the Class V220, were made. It was this class that was the inspiration behind the construction of the D800 'Warship' diesel-hydraulics for British Railways Western Region at Swindon in 1960. The extremely heavy maintenance costs on this type of locomotive meant that although it continued to be used in Germany, the technology was not widely exported to railways elsewhere in the world.

Above: A Southern Pacific No. 4001 seen here hauling freight.

Right: Built by General Motors Electro-Motive Division, the four axles of the 'F' type were all powered in a Bo–Bo configuration. Used for both passenger and freight services, the 'F' originally stood for <u>F</u>ifteen hundred horsepower and not for 'freight', as has been frequently misinterpreted.

BY THE 1950s THE PROCESS of dieselisation was well in progress in the United States. At the beginning of World War II there had been over 40,000 steam locomotives at work on US railroads, but a little over a decade later, this total had decreased to just over 15,000. On 1 January 1948 Britain's railways were nationalised, but no attempt was made to embrace the new diesel revolution. This situation changed drastically with the publication of the 1955 Modernisation Plan, which put forward a strategy to sweep away steam in Britain. Most historians are agreed that the plan was an ill-conceived attempt to emulate American successes which proved, in the short term, to be disastrous.

Above: A British Railways Class 47 Co–Co Diesel Electric waits to leave Liverpool Lime Street with a locomotive hauled cross-country service. These cross-country workings, hauled by Class 47s, which date back to 1962 constituted some of the last locomotive hauled trains left in British service.

British Railways

Whilst there was no doubt that many of the steam locomotives in service with British Railways were outdated and inefficient. The plan meant that many engines that had been constructed in more recent times, such as the BR Standard classes, were sent for scrap long before the end of their intended working lives. In other parts of Europe, such as France and Germany, a much more strategic approach was taken, with steam being phased out gradually over a number of years. Steam was eliminated from BR by 1968, whereas in Germany it continued until 1975.

British Railways were unwilling to utilise American technology and home builders were used to construct the new diesel fleet, with somewhat mixed results. In 1955, the first of the 'Deltic' class was built by English Electric at the Vulcan Foundry. Subsequently, 22 examples of this class were built for use on the East Coast Main Line. Three years after the appearance of *Deltic*, the independently minded Western Region decided to adopt hydraulic transmission rather than electric and so the North British Locomotive Company built the first diesel-hydraulic locomotive for BR.

The D600 class, which was unreliable, underpowered and therefore short-lived, was followed by the more powerful D800 series 'Warship' and 'Western' classes. In all, Swindon introduced six diesel-hydraulic classes of over 300 locomotives. By 1977 they had all been withdrawn, the cost of maintenance ruling out their widespread use on British Railways. Some of the diesel-electric designs introduced by BR, such as the Class 47 which first appeared in 1962 and built both at Crewe Works

and by Brush Traction, numbered over 500, are still in use today.

Russia

It was the introduction of American-built locomotives during World War II that initiated the beginning of the diesel age in the former Soviet Union. Russian designs evolved from the study of Alco and Baldwin locomotives, and what followed was a gradual evolution. The first diesel-electric engine, the TE1, was built in 1945, with a much

DIESEL REPLACES STEAM

larger, 4,000hp locomotive appearing in 1953. This was a double unit, over 2,000 of which were constructed, including further modified versions for passenger use.

The Third World

Throughout the world, particularly in Africa and South America, the onset of diesel traction has been patchy. In a race to modernise their countries, many Third World nations bought diesels, but found that spares, skilled labour and other factors

meant they were not the bargain they thought they would be. Nevertheless, many countries without their own manufacturers relied heavily on imported locomotives, largely from the United States and the former communist block. In countries such as China and South Africa, however, the growth of diesel traction was limited by the rich reserves of coal and other natural resources, which meant that steam locomotives lingered on much longer than in other places. Important though the introduction of diesels has been in many countries, it has been the onset of electrification that has had the most dramatic effect on railway operation.

Above: Diesels came late to the former USSR and it was not until the 1950s that they really began to take hold. Used mainly for freight-haulage, the T Class was one of Russia's most prolific diesel types, with a total production of over 2,000.

ELECTRIFICATION

Above: **With its booming post-war economy a high-investment Japan has led the way in urban electrification.**

Railway, opened in 1883, but it was not until 1890 that electrification was introduced more generally into railway operation.

Suburban Electrification

It was in large cities that electrified railways first took hold; the fumes and smoke generated by steam locomotives meant that this new form of traction was ideal. In December 1890, the City & South London, the world's first underground electric railway, opened for business, followed three years later by the Liverpool Overhead Railway, the first elevated city railway. This 525V dc system was quickly followed by electric railways in many urban areas, particularly in the United States where, in the early 20th century, they were built in New York, Boston, Philadelphia and Chicago. In Britain, other suburban systems, such as those on Tyneside, linking Newcastle and Benton, and the Lancashire Line from Liverpool to Southport, were opened in 1904.

Both these British lines used a 600V dc system picking up current from a third rail, and it was this that was eventually adopted by one of the largest electrified suburban systems in the world. When the Southern Railway was created after Grouping in 1923, it found that it had inherited three competing electric railways, all with different systems of operation. The 'Elevated Electric', of the old London, Brighton & South Coast Railway, used overhead catenary wires, whereas the South Eastern Railway and the London & South Western Railway both used conductor rails. After some consideration it was decided to adopt the third rail 600 volt arrangement since it was cheaper to install and maintain. It was also more suited to commuter railways where short journeys with frequent stops were the norm. Ultimately the Southern Railway's electrification scheme spread far beyond the tangle of lines around South London, and the routes from London to Brighton, and London to Portsmouth became part of the 'Southern Electric' system. That the Southern had acquired three different forms of electrified railway typified the approach in the early years.

High Voltage

The low voltage dc system used on the Southern, and other mainly suburban railways such as the

THE FIRST TENTATIVE STEPS towards railway electrification were made in 1879, when Werner von Siemens demonstrated a 1,000mm gauge electric railway at the Berlin Trades Exhibition. Although only capable of travelling at 4mph (6.4kph) this development was the start of a process which continues in Europe today with the network of high-speed railways that crosses the continent. Siemens' railway was demonstrated all over Europe, whilst in the United States Thomas Edison experimented with electric traction, setting up the Electric Company of America in 1883 – the predecessor of the General Electric Corporation. Small experimental schemes, such as Volks Railway on Brighton beach and the Giant's Causeway

New York Central, was largely superseded by a high voltage 3-phase ac power source. Between 1901 and 1903 German engineers working for Siemens and AEG had tested a train running on 10,000 volt 3-phase which, in October 1903, reached a record speed of 135mph (217kph). This method was used in Switzerland in 1906 on the Burgdorf to Thun line and subsequently on services through the Gotthard Tunnel.

In nearby Italy 3-phase ac was also used widely. The E550 class of engines built by the Italian State Railways from 1908 onwards, to climb the ferocious gradients of the Giovi pass near Genoa, showed, even at this early date, the benefits of electrification. Although half the size of the steam locomotives they replaced, they cut journey times by nearly 50 per cent.

Elsewhere, before World War I, different systems were introduced, as many railway companies and manufacturers experimented with this brave new technology. In Canada the Canadian Northern Railroad employed 2,400V dc catenary wires, whilst in France they used a lower voltage of 1,500V. It would not be until after the World War I that a more coherent pattern of electrification would emerge.

Above: Some of the early electrified lines were those involving rack and pinion mountain railways, Switzerland and Austria having the best examples.

Left: Sitting below the tangled maze of overhead lines of the 25kV ac system at Manchester's Piccadilly Station is a class 323 of North Western Trains partnered on the right by a Class 158 diesel.

Switzerland

After the First World War, electrification continued to spread throughout Europe, but there was still with some disagreement over the method to be used. Switzerland led the way, and its rapid adoption of electric traction, whilst partly due to the lack of coal reserves, also related to the steeply graded alpine lines, which tested steam locomotives to their limit. One of the earliest lines electrified, the Gotthard route, was tackled because the Gotthard Tunnel frequently became choked with smoke. The Simplon Tunnel faced the same problems, and so was also equipped with 3-phase ac Brown–Boveri locomotives from its inception in 1906. Swiss engineers had also been experimenting with single-phase ac electrification, and this had been tried on the Seebach–Wettingham line two years earlier. This system used only one catenary wire, was more reliable and gave more flexible speed control than 3-phase.

The Seebach experiment was short-lived, but after World War I, the first two engines used on the line were pressed into service on the route from Lucerne through the Gotthard Tunnel into Italy. The old 3-phase system was replaced by single-phase 15,000V, a standard that was to be adopted subsequently on all Swiss main line railways. The motley selection of motive power used when the line opened in 1920, was replaced in 1922 when Swiss Railways were supplied with 40 Class Be 4/6 engines built by Brown–Boveri.

Italy

Italy, which had begun electrification before World War I, became one of the leading exponents of this form of traction in the inter-war period. Although continuing with 3-phase technology in the 1920s, it had adopted 3,000V dc as a standard by the end of the decade. Like Switzerland, Italy did not have substantial coal reserves, but it did have plentiful hydroelectric power.

When Benito Mussolini came to power, the electrification of the state railway network came to symbolise the progress made by his fascist regime. Coupled with improvements in locomotive technology, Italian State Railways also built new lines known as 'Direttissima' that bypassed old steeply graded lines that transformed routes between major cities. On 20 July 1939, an ETR inter-city train made the fastest rail journey then on record when it travelled from Florence to Milan at an average speed of 102mph (164kph).

Scandinavia

Hydroelectric power was also plentiful in Scandinavian countries, and thus electrification also made great progress there before World War II. In Sweden, experiments took place before the state railway settled on the 15,000V single-phase European system favoured by Switzerland. In 1923 the Lapland line was converted, and two years later the main line from Gothenburg to Stockholm was similarly treated. The Class D locomotive built for passenger working, became a standard design and were built in one form or another with increasing power, from 1925 to 1957.

Europe

Single-phase, 15,000 volt systems were also introduced in Austria, Belgium and Germany, although in the latter country steam still retained some influence. In France much the same situation prevailed, with steam not being supplanted until after the Second World War. It was only the Southern Railway in Britain that pursued electrification with any real enthusiasm. The staunchly conservative Great Western Railway did investigate the electrification of the Paddington to Penzance line west of Taunton in the 1930s, but the proposals came to nothing. Even today, the former GWR network is the least electrified in the country. On the LNER, apart from the electrification of ex-Great Eastern lines north of London, the main scheme was the conversion of the Sheffield to Manchester route, a project which was interrupted by the outbreak of World War II and not completed until 1954. Like France, Britain was not easily seduced by the benefits of electric traction, and was still firmly in love with the steam locomotive.

Left: A north-bound express negotiates the southern approaches to Crewe on Britain's West Coast main line. This entire 400-mile route from London, Euston, to Glasgow is electrified to 25kV ac. One of the route's principal types is this Class 87 Bo–Bo electrics, introduced in 1973.

Below: Anshan is China's steel capital. The area is surrounded by rich deposits of iron ore and a circular electric railway, which encompasses the town works, brings the ore from the outlying mines. The 1,500V dc line has a fascinating variety of locomotives and this example is seen at the base of the huge Dagushan open cast mine to the south of the city. No. 051 is a Bo–Bo–Bo, which utilises both overhead and side contact.

ELECTRIFICATION – A WORLD REVOLUTION

SINCE WORLD WAR II, improvements in technology have made a great impact on the electrification of world railway systems. In the early 1950s the introduction of a single-phase 25,000 volt (25kV) system on the Aix-Les-Bains and La Roche-sur-Foron line persuaded railway companies in many countries to adopt this form of electric traction. In 1956, two years after the 1,500V Manchester to Sheffield route had been opened, British Railways decided to adopt 25kV 50hz as standard for future installations. The first trains using this system in Britain began running between Colchester and Clacton in 1959.

More substantial electrification took place in the early 1960s, when the West Coast Main Line between Euston and the North West was completed. The line from the Capital to Manchester and Liverpool commenced electric operation in April 1966 and was completed through to Glasgow in 1974. The electrification of the East Coast Main Line from King's Cross to Edinburgh was not completed until July 1991. It had been hoped to use the ill-fated APT (Advanced Passenger Train) on this and the West Coast route, but its failure led to new Class 90 and 91 locomotives and rolling stock being produced.

France

The adoption of 25kV did not mean the wholesale scrapping of the 1,500V system that had already been installed on some lines in this country. The development of locomotives capable of switching between voltages meant that interchangeability across railways and borders was possible. In 1994, SNCF still had over 3,000 miles (4,800km) of 1,500V lines compared with over 4,000 miles (6,400km) of 25kV. The most dramatic development in France was the introduction of the famous TGV. In September 1981, these 25kV high speed trains inaugurated a service between Paris and Lyon, covering the 265 miles (426km) in 2 hours. Capable of speeds up to 187.5mph (300kph) they have revolutionised European rail transport. TGV technology has heavily influenced the design of rolling stock used for the operation of the Channel Tunnel. Eurostar trains, built by GEC–Alsthom in France can run on 25kV, 1,500V and 750V dc third rail lines and are capable of speeds comparable with the TGV. The combination of Eurostar and TGV trains has meant that travel between Britain and

Europe has become much faster; the only remaining obstacle now is the construction of the direct high speed link between London and the Channel Tunnel.

China

The changes in Europe have been mirrored elsewhere in the world, and electrification is seen as the long-term goal for many railways. The Oil Crisis of the 1970s has merely served to emphasise the fragility of dependence on fossil fuels, and even countries with substantial mineral reserves have been taking great strides towards electrification of their railway systems. China, which used steam power long after many other countries, is now adopting electric traction. Its first main line to be electrified was the Cheng Tu–Paochi route that opened in July 1975. It too uses the 25kV system, and in 1994 had over 5,000 miles (8,000km) of electrified track. However, here is still a great deal of work to be done since the Chinese rail network is around 33,000 miles (53,000km)!

Japan

Perhaps the most striking adoption of electrification has been in nearby Japan, where the construction of the Shinkansen 'Bullet' trains have caught the imagination of not only the Japanese, but the whole world. The route linking Tokyo and Osaka was revolutionary since it was an entirely new line bypassing the old 3ft 6in gauge network. Since the 1970s further 25kV 'Shinkansen' routes have been opened, with the country's railway network being brought together by tunnels and bridges that have linked a multitude of Japanese islands. The 200mph (322kph) 'Bullet' trains and the technology that created them are a stirring advertisement for the benefits of electric traction and the future direction of railways.

Right: This experimental streamlined high-speed Bo–Bo–De-4–De electric was produced by the German firm of Henschel in 1982, for the Deutsche Bundesbahn.

Below: Rigging the overhead wires of the electrification scheme.

8 Railways *in* *the* **INDUSTRIAL** Revolution

COLLIERY RAILWAYS

BY THE MID-1800s COLLIERY railways had become as much a part of the landscape as had train whistles in the night. A special factor in these vast networks was the constricted confines of the colliery layouts which often prohibited the use of larger main line engines for colliery trains, the preferred type being the 0–6–0T.

Britain

A good example of a colliery railway was at Ashington in North East England. Opened in 1850, a railway connection was soon made with the North Eastern Railway's main line at Blyth, from where the coal was exported to countries such as Germany, Poland and Sweden. Ashington was also a principal supplier of 'steam coal' which was sent to locomotive sheds all over Britain. By the mid-1930s the company possessed 15 route miles (24km) of railway along with 9 miles (14.5km) of sidings that gave a storage capacity for some 35,000 tons of coal in wagons. A total of 750 wagons was owned by the colliery along with 17 steam locomotives.

Colliery Passenger Trains

Some of the bigger colliery complexes in Britain also ran workman's passenger trains to coincide with the various shifts. Using second-hand rolling stock, some of these trains made fascinating sights with their vintage coaches from old main line companies and including such antiques as ex-North Eastern clerestories, ex–Furness curved tops, and ex-Great Northern directors' saloons. At first, some collieries made their trains available to all members of the community, although with nationalisation these were put on a non-fare paying basis and confined to colliery employees. By the early 1900s there were hundreds of collieries in Britain, many with their own railway but it is many years since a colliery has operated such a passenger service.

Europe and the Rest of the World

Although Britain had by far the most collieries, specialised coal operations were also very important in Europe, especially the German Ruhrgebiet, Russia and Poland. In some parts of the world, notably South Africa with its steeply undulating branch lines,

larger engines than were used in Europe, up to 4–8–2s, were needed to work over connections that were more like branch lines in their own right. In Australia, with its vast areas, coal field trains were often worked by down-graded main line tender engines. Conversely, in India it is interesting that the 2ft gauge (610mm) railways of the Assam collieries used even smaller engines than in Britain with saddle tanks of 0–4–0 and 0–4–2 wheel arrangements being common. The vast colliery complex around Asansol, on the other hand, is operated by 5ft 6in gauge main line engines under contract to the coal holdings.

North America and China

From the beginning, coal mine lines have played an important role in railroading in the United States. At one time there were many lines, mostly narrow gauge running below ground conveying coal products to the surface, as in other countries. These railways were found in Pennsylvania, West Virginia, Colorado, Utah and elsewhere. In later years many of these railways were electrified. While coal remains an important commodity for the main line carriers, few of the coal mine railways survive as they have been largely supplanted by other means of extracting coal from the ground.

The huge Chinese coal fields have for many years, been mostly worked by tender engines and, in more recent decades, by the standard SY class 2–8–2s, built at Tangshan. What a fascinating contrast these giants make with the classic 0–6–0 colliery engines used in Britain. China is the last bastion of the colliery railway and it can be said with confidence, that there will still be colliery steam trains at work in China in 2013 – two centuries after the world's first examples appeared in Northumberland.

Above: The most celebrated locomotive type in British industrial history was the Hunslet Austerity, which was built for service during World War II. The first was steamed at Hunslet's works on 1 January 1943. Having played an important part during the war, both in Britain and Europe, many passed to the newly emergent National Coal Board. The type continued to be built for industrial service until as late as 1964, by which time a grand total of 484 engines had been reached.

Below: An afternoon Miners' Special approaches the Chislet Colliery, Halt on the Kent coalfield. The train is hauled by an LMS-designed Fairburn 2–6–4T.

IRON AND STEEL INDUSTRIES

Above: A scene at Anshan Iron and Steel Works, the largest in China with an incredible steel-making capacity of 10 million tons a year. Some 50 steam locomotives work throughout the complex. Here one of the standard Chinese-built SY class 2–8–2s waits to draw ladles of molten iron from one of the blast furnaces.

BY DEFINITION, RAILWAYS and iron ore are compatible bedfellows on account of the sheer weight that has to be carried. The first locomotive for use on an iron ore railway system is believed to be that which started work at Irthlingborough in Northamptonshire in 1867.

Britain

Today, the industry in Britain is extinct. The decline in the demand for home ore has been partly due to the high cost of transportation and partly because the iron content was only 28–30 per cent, whereas imported Swedish ore was up to 65 per cent.

One of Britain's most fascinating ironstone related railways was centred on the South East Midland's steel town of Corby. The works had their own railway that fanned out in a huge network of branches into the verdant countryside to bring the ore from the various pits. In the 1950s, Corby had a large fleet of tank engines for its mines division and another for its steel works. Apart from feeding the local steel works, the Northamptonshire iron ore beds supplied ore to other great steel areas. At its peak, as many as ten train loads a day could be seen threading their way northwards bound for the great steel works of Yorkshire and Nottinghamshire.

Austria

Undoubtedly one of the most fascinating steam-operated lines in the world was the Erzberg, or 'Iron Mountain Railway'. This standard gauge line conveys iron ore from the 2,400ft (731m) high mountain to the steel works at Donawitz. Opened in 1891, one of the many fascinating aspects of this 12½-mile long railway is the use of both rack and adhesion traction. Much of the route has a ruling gradient of 1 in 14 over which 0–6–2Ts hauled loads of up to 110 tons. The line's original locomotives were 0–6–2, 4-cylinder rack and adhesion tank engines, built by the Wiener Lokomotivfabrik at Floridsdorf between 1890 and 1908.

Australia

In 1932, with the establishment of a steelworks at Port Kembla in New South Wales, a railway was constructed up the steep mountainsides to connect the industrial area with the main line at Moss Vale. The new line, approximately 43½ miles (70km) in length, was one of the longest industrial lines in the world.

China

One of the most spectacular iron and steel operations to be found anywhere is centred round Anshan where, apart from abundant coal reserves, there are also vast iron ore deposits. The quarries are linked to the city's steel works by a circular electric railway which, as well as serving the various mines, also operates a passenger service. This is primarily to service the needs of the huge workforce, the entire operation employing more than 250,000 peope. It is fascinating to think that this railway runs electric locomotives that are much older than the steam engines on the Chinese railway network. The railway network reaches every nook and cranny of the complex. Divided into twelve railway control areas, at any one time there are over 100 locomotives in use on the 15 'main lines' from which many branches diverge.

North America

American steel mills usually operate complex internal rail networks in and around their plants. Often, these lines are standard gauge and capable of interchanging freight cars with the connecting common-carrier rail lines. While in recent years most of these lines have been diesel powered, North Western Steel & Wire, located at Sterling, Illinois continued to operate steam locomotives until 1980, decades after most other lines had retired steam from regular service. At some plants special rail equipment was used to transport molten steel from one facility to another. With the decline of the steel industry in the United States, many mills have shut down, thus eliminating the need for these specialised railways, yet in the late 1990s there are still a few of these lines operating.

Above: Deep amid the jungle of Bihar lie the world's biggest deposits of iron-ore – an estimated 2½ thousand million tons, which is believed to be 60% iron in content. Here, a brace of Andrew Barclay 0–4–2 tanks thread a rake of iron-ore through jungle on their way to the Indian Railway's south-eaStern main line.

Left: The last steam-worked ironstone mine in Britain was at Nassington, Northamptonshire. Here, deep in the gullet, two 16-inch (406MM) Hunslet 0–6–0 saddle tanks wait to take a trainload of ore to the connection with the British Railway main line. Note the dynamited ore strata in the left foreground and the deep gullet from which the ironstone is being taken. With an iron content as low as 30%, these fields were considered uneconomical when compared with imported ores of up to 70% iron content.

Right: Calcutta Docks took the unusual step of standardising their locomotive fleet with 45 of these 0–6–2 Tanks, which first came from the Hunslet works in Leeds in 1945. Later engines came from the German builder Henschel of Kassel and Mitsubitsi of Japan. Having chosen an ideal type of locomotive, the port authority resisted all temptations to diversify and achieved a tremendous economy of operation.

HARBOURS, DOCKS AND SHIPYARDS

HARBOURS AND RAILWAYS have an inevitably close association. Although some main line trains went right into the docks area, many ports had separate internal rail systems that formed an intrinsic bridge between land and sea, transferring goods and materials between ships and the main lines. Dockside locomotives had to be smaller than their main line sisters as they often had to negotiate constricted areas where conventional engines could not go. Because of these confined spaces, tanks of modest proportions were usually used. Perhaps the most dramatic exception to the norm were the massive 2–10–2 tank enginess belonging to the Bombay Port Trust that were used for hump shunting. These worked alongside more traditional engines in the form of a batch of delightful 2–6–0 tanks from Nasmyth Wilson of Manchester. The subcontinent's other large port, Calcutta, used a fleet of 0–6–2 tanks. The large American seaports, such as New York, San Francisco and Oakland, had complex networks of waterfront trackwork and car float operations. These lines were usually standard gauge and capable of interchange with main line railways. As waterfront railways often involved a considerable amount of street running with the rails set in the roadway and with unusually tight curvature and narrow clearances, lightweight switch engines were usually employed. These lines were one of the first places where diesel electric locomotives were used, although the Brooklyn Eastern District continued to operate steam until the 1960s – notably later than on similar lines elsewhere.

Shipyards

Most shipyards received the materials necessary for shipbuilding in sections by rail, which was then transferred by the company's internal railway to the various prefabrication shops in the yard. A case in point is that of Doxford's shipyard at Sunderland which was reconstructed in the early 1900s to a layout containing 13 miles (21km) of track, based on the use of steam crane locomotives. The first of these, built by Hawthorn, Leslie of Newcastle upon Tyne, were in service by 1904. Able to lift weights of up to 4 tons they saw service for nearly 70 years before being retired in 1971. This was due to various factors, such as the lack of spare parts as well as the introduction of Sunderland's smokeless zone policy. Indeed, Doxford's whole railway network was dispensed with and roads were laid over the trackbeds, this modernisation of handling methods bringing about the demise of the crane tanks. This type of engine had tended to flower in the shipyards where bulky and awkwardly shaped loads had to be handled, but were superseded by fork-lift trucks and more mobile road cranes.

Heavy industrial ship building only occurred in a few places and it has been said that in the late 19th/early 20th century, four out of every five ships on the oceans of the world came from Glasgow yards. It was here on Clydeside, that the distinctive Scottish 0–4–0 saddle tank, known locally as 'pugs' flitted between the gloomy structures of the docks. Other major shipyards with extensive rail systems included Belfast, Malmo, Gdansk, Hamburg, Kiel and Rostock where the classic German industrial shunters were features of the industrial landscape.

Building of Harbours and Sea Defences

In many parts of the world, railways were used in the construction of the harbours with contractors' engines being common. Once built these harbours sometimes provided an ongoing use for railways to maintain breakwaters. In the case of Holyhead and Ponta del Garda in the mid-Atlantic islands of the Azores, the use of the rare 7ft gauge was employed. In the Azores, broad gauge trains brought boulders from nearby quarries and piled them onto the sea wall. However, as fast as they were piled up, the rocks were washed out to sea by the Atlantic breakers! It is sobering to think that the last vestige of Brunel's broad gauge dream ended on a breakwater in the middle of the Atlantic Ocean.

Below: One of the Crane Tanks which worked at Sunderland's Doxford Shipyard on the River Wear until the early 1970s. The engine is named *Roker* and was built by Robert Stephenson & Hawthorn of Newcastle-upon-Tyne as an 0–4–0 Crane Tank. These were the last Crane Tanks to remain in service in Britain and among the last in the world.

LOGGING RAILWAYS

Because of the transient nature of timber harvesting these lines were often lightly built, with sharp curves and often very steep climbs of up to 10 and 15 per cent in some situations. In the steam era, specialized geared locomotives were used to negotiate the rough track of these steep winding lines. The most popular type of locomotive was the Shay which was built by Lima, and used a row of vertical cylinders to power a cranked shaft. Logging railways had a variety of specialized cars to move raw timber, including free wheel sets without frames that could be attached to large logs for movement over the rails. Logging railways were once found in northern New England, the central Appalachian region including Pennsylvania, West Virginia and Kentucky, the Sierra mountains of California and the Cascade region of the Pacific North West. Today, only a handful of these logging lines remain.

Shay Articulated Locomotives

The spectacular nature of a logging railway gave birth to a number of distinctive articulated locomotive types, the most famous of which was the Shay. First introduced in 1880 as the brainchild of Ephraim Shay, a Michigan logging engineer, the idea was adopted by the Lima locomotive works of Ohio. Built predominantly for home use, the majority were standard gauge, although a few narrow gauge examples were exported, most notably to Taiwan, the Philippines, Australia and South America. In the Philippines, the Insular Lumber Company on Negros Island operated a remote 3ft 6in gauge logging line that carried teak from mountain forests down to the sawmills that were at sea level. After bringing the logs down, the train stopped on a ledge and the logs were mechanically pushed off of the wagons and allowed to crash into the artificial lake far below.

The Feldbahn

A wonderful contrast to the Shays were the Feldbahns. Some of these famous veterans of World War I ended up as logging engines, the last survivors being at Czarna Bialostoka, a 75-mile (120km) long forestry system close to Bialystok, on the main line from Warsaw to St Petersburg. This system is now operated by diesels which are built in the former East German city of Karl Marx Stadt,

Above: China has many forestry railways, especially in the north-east of the country. Many of these lines are of 762mm gauge and use a standard type of 28-ton 0–8–0, which is based on a Russian design built prolifically in both Eastern Europe and China itself. This scene is on the system radiating from Lanxiang and shows the morning workmen's passenger train pausing at Juan Jie station. Notice how the loaded cars on the right are formed of free-moving bogie units, so allowing them to take trunks of any length.

ALMOST FROM THE BEGINNING of railways trains have been used to haul timber, and over the years, a wide variety of logging operations has evolved. The most ideal is the felling of trees near the developing rail track, but invariably this is not practicable and logs have to be carried to a point of contact with the railway. A variety of methods have been used, such as rolling the logs down slopes, dragging them with mechanical or animal traction, or floating them down rivers. As with other 'heavy' industrial railways, logging has declined greatly; not because the demand for the commodity has decreased, as has coal and iron, but because most logging is based around heavy trucking which, at best, takes the logs to the nearest main line railhead or, at worst, to the ultimate destination.

USA

The American Pacific North West is one of the most important logging areas of the world. American timber companies used logging railways to haul raw logs from the forest to the saw mills and the cut lumber products to main line railroad connections.

which has now reverted to its prepartition name of Chemniz.

Puerto Castado, Paraguay

One of the most fascinating logging areas in the world is the Paraguayan Chacao where the quebracho tree, once the major source of tannin, grows. The logs are transported by rail from the forests to the huge factory that dominates the town of Puerto Castado. The factory processes the logs into tannin, after which it makes an incredible river journey on barges to Buenos Aires, from where it is exported.

China

In more recent times, a vast logging industry has opened up in North China where innumerable 760mm gauge railways, using 28 ton locomotives, convey the logs over vast distances to the main line network. The logs are then carried down through Manchuria on huge freight trains to Peking and the great China beyond.

Above: The Insular Lumber Company's incredible four-cylinder compound 0–6–6–0 Mallet, built by Baldwins of Philadelphia, in the mid-1920s, eases a rake of mahogany logs onto a wooden trestle viaduct, built in the classic Wild Western manner under American colonial rule. An active volcano adorns the backdrop.

Below: Winching logs into wagons of China's main line trains in the exchange yard at Lanxiang. These logs are destined to be conveyed down the main lines of Manchuria for use throughout China.

Right: A battered ALCO-built Mogul of the early 1920s arrives at a cane-loading siding at the Ma Ao sugar central on the Phillipine island of Negros. A cart-load of cane makes a timely arrival behind a water buffalo – known locally as *Caribaos*.

SUGAR IS A WORLD INDUSTRY and as soon as sugar plantations were developed in various parts of the world railways were seen as the most logical means of moving the vast tonnages as quickly as possible. This rapid transportation of the cane, which grows from 15 to 20ft (4.5 to 6m) high, is important for, when cut, the leaden cane rapidly loses moisture and thus sugar content.

Sugar Cane

Many of the principal sugar cane producing countries have made extensive use of railways as a link between plantation and factory and extensive railway operations are to be found in Brazil, Cuba, Mauritius, Australia, the Philippines, Java, Fiji, and India.

Java

With over 50 active sugar factories, Java provides an excellent example as to how prolific these sugar networks can be. Some of these factories are interconnected and provide one of the most fascinating steam networks in the word today. Although 700mm gauge railways predominate, some factories are laid to 600mm. Each of these systems has a number of lines fanning outwards in different directions from the factory with an average total of about 50 miles (80km) of track. Operations within a system are seldom dull, and apart from the continuous hauls from the plantations, there is much factory shunting and trip working.

In Java, as in parts of India and the Philippines, sugar field railways are self-sufficient inasmuch as they burn bagasse. This is the natural waste product

loading sidings that receive at least one daily visit by a steam-worked train.

Although all sugar plantation railway systems are even in their own way vast operations, in Cuba they are more dramatic. Here, many medium-sized 'main line' type engines, some bought second-hand from American railroads, haul cane over long distances and frequently traverse sections of the country's national railway as part of the route between plantation and factory.

Mozambique

One small, but prolific, sugar line is that of the Sena Sugar Estates in Mozambique, South-East Africa. This British-owned concern connects with the trans–Zambesi Railway which links Malawi and Nyasaland with Mozambique.

Sugar Beet

Sugar railways were not only confined to tropical plantations but also found favour in the austere climes of Europe as sugar-beet railways. Sugar was first extracted from beet in 1747 and the first sugar-beet factory in the world was established in Silesia in 1801. There is no difference between the sugar content of cane and beet – both contain 90–98 per cent sucrose (99 per cent after refining). Almost one third of world sugar from beet is produced in Europe and the United States and, unlike cane, is mainly grown for domestic consumption.

In California and Oregon, sugar beets are transported to large processing mills in specially designed cars. Traditionally, these sugar mills also operated their own railways.

An example of a European main beet growing area which had its own railway network is England's East Anglia. The tank locomotives used at Peterborough Sugar Factory were the model for 'Thomas the tank engine' – probably the most well-known fictional locomotive in world literature. On its retirement from active service in 1971, the last sugar-beet engine in England was preserved. It has since been painted blue, given a face, and has delighted countless children ever since.

Below: A scene at the sugar mill of the Hawaiian Philippine Company, one of the largest sugar concerns on the Philippine island of Negros. The factory yard is shunted by a brace of Baldwin-built 0–6–2 saddle tanks, which were transferred to Negros from the company's interests in Hawaii.

of the cane and although its calorific value is abysmally low, the dry fibres, when baled, provide fuel free of cost. Because an awful lot is needed to go a short distance tender–tank engines predominate throughout the plantations.

USA and Cuba

On the Hawaiian islands, sugar cane railways were once used to haul cane to the processing plants. While these lines have largely been abandoned or converted to tourist railways, similar operations can still be found in Cuba, an island once controlled by the United States. Cuban sugar locomotives are larger and oil is the preferred fuel for the increased steam pressure required. The cane is brought by animal-hauled carts to the

POWER STATIONS AND GASWORKS

Above: A typically heavy-duty 0–6–0 Side Tank in British industrial service working for the Central Electricity Generating Board.

Right: A heavy-duty 4–8–2 side tank delivers coal to the power station adjacent to the New Largo Colliery in South Africa's Transvaal. Many of these large Glasgow-built engines, along with a 4–8–4 version, could be found in industrial service at collieries and electricity generating stations in the Transvaal.

Thermal Power Stations

IT IS INTERESTING to reflect that a considerable percentage of the world's electricity is still generated by steam – including that which goes to run electrified railway main lines. In spite of this, most power station railway systems have long since been converted from steam to diesel power or, more likely, to the modern concept of diesel or electrically operated 'merry-go-round' trains. Thermal power stations have always demanded lots of coal, but those that survive (by definition the largest ones) demand even more coal to generate the steam that drives the turbines which, in turn, generate the electricity.

The steam locomotive played an important part in the railway operation of the electricity industry, both before and after nationalisation in the late 1940s. Large numbers of steam locomotives, mostly 0–4–0 and 0–6–0 side and saddle tank types, were employed on the thankless daily task of moving thousands of tons of high quality steam coal from the railhead and reception yards to the boiler houses at the many power stations in Britain and the former Empire.

Traditionally, many power stations have been connected directly with local collieries, a perfect example being the vast thermal plant at Korba, in India's Madhya Pradesh, which is linked with the col-

liery at Manikpur, some 10 miles (16km) distant, by means of its own railway system.

The power station locomotive, which hauls the coal from the connections with the main line railway, reduces the formations into manageable length trains of several wagons before conveying them to the furnaces of the power station boilers. Once emptied, the industrial engine then reassembles the wagons at the exchange siding leaving them ready to be conveyed back to the colliery by main line traffic.

Many power station locomotives, usually saddle tanks, were used to take loaded coal wagons from the reception sidings with the main line and place them on off-loading roads. From here they rolled by gravity, onto the tipplers adjacent to the main boiler plants.

In recent later years power stations have reduced in number and those that have remained are much larger and newer, making merry-go-round trains more viable. These are worked by the main line locomotive which hauls the full length train slowly through the plant while the wagons are emptied, one at a time, automatically. The progression to nuclear and oil-fired power stations has done away with the need for an internal railway system at such plants.

Gasworks

Prior to the exploitation of natural gas, the humble gasworks played a vital role in energising the nation. Yet again, here is another classic 'industrial revolution' activity which has all but vanished in favour of increasing use of electricity and the utilisation of natual gas pipe lines. Gasworks were dependent on voluminous amounts of coal, all of which was brought in by rail.

The gas industry had its origins in the late 1830s when, for the first, time coal gas was manufactured for domestic lighting, heating and for use in industry. Also, other by-products were produced at gasworks including coke and coal tar which was used in the pharmaceutical and construction industries.

In order to transport these products, both in and out of city gasworks, railways were used in abundance. Probably the largest such railway operation anywhere in the world was at Beckton in East London, England, where a network of up to 90 or more miles (145km) of track was to be found. In order to service this system a class of small 0–4–0 side tank engines was especially designed and built by Neilson Reid of Glasgow. These locomotives ran in everyday service from the early 1880s until the mid-1960s when they were withdrawn. At least three examples are preserved in museums.

The railways and their equipment came in all shapes and sizes and a multitude of gauges both in Britain and the Empire, however, after the British gas industry was nationalised in the late 1940s various standard classes of 0–6–0 and 0–4–0 saddle and side tank started to replace the myriad of types that had done sterling work for the previous 100 years in these smokey establishments.

Below: The last steam-worked colliery in Britain was at Cadley Hill, near Burton-upon-Trent, on the Derbyshire Coalfield. This 1981 scene brings to an end the 175-year long partnership between steam and coal, the life-blood of the industrial revolution. The colliery served the distant Drakelow Power Station seen in the background. The locomotives are right – a Hunslet Austerity 0–6–0 saddle tank and left – an 0–6–0 saddle tank, built by Robert Stephenson & Hawthorn of Newcastle.

AGRICULTURAL AND PEAT INDUSTRIES

RAILWAYS WERE NOT CONFINED to the inherent elements of the industrial landscape but saw prolific use in the countryside. Apart from sugar, which has been covered separately, some of the more interesting commodities transported by rail have included cotton, jute, esparto grass, palm oil, potatoes, ground nuts and peat.

Cotton and Jute

In the case of cotton, the most prolific operation in the world is the Gezira Project in the Sudan. Radiating from the Wad El Shafie, the British inspired, 600mm gauge Gezira railway system features Hunslet 0–8–0 diesel locomotives.

Railways for carrying jute have been built, most notably in India. Here, as in munitions plants and paper mills, the type of locomotive chosen is the fireless steam engine which takes its steam supply from a static source. Sparks from a conventional steam locomotive would wreak havoc on the dry plants.

Palm Oil

The main industry of Tanjungbalai, in Sumatra, is that of palm oil which is used in the manufacture of soap and margarine. Enormous tonnages of fruit are conveyed from the plantations to the mills on various steam-operated narrow gauge railway systems. These lines radiate outwards from the factories into the plantations and are operated by 0–4–4–0T Mallets built by the Dutch firm of Ducroo & Brauns. The hard kernel shells, which are the natural waste products of the palm oil process, are not wasted and are used as locomotive fuel. These nut shells are high in calorific value, unlike the bagasse used on the sugar railways of neighbouring Java.

Potatoes and Ground Nuts

The famous potato railways of Argentina were part of the former Buenos Aires & Great Southern Railway (BAGS). They consisted of a network of 2ft gauge lines which used former World War I Hunslet 4–6–0s which had been rendered surplus following the cessation of hostilities. That such operations existed underscores the immense tonnage of foodstuffs borne by Argentina's railways at a time when the country was the 'world's larder' and one of the world's leading economies. In the later years Simplex petrol and diesel locomotives were employed.

On the other side of the world, in Africa, groundnut railways were built as extensions from the metre gauge main lines found in Kenya and Uganda. These were the inspiration of the British Colonial Office and, although they operated for a while, proved to be economically unviable and were short-lived.

Peat

One of the most remarkable and extensive industrial railway operations in the world operates in the Irish Republic. As there are no coal deposits in Ireland, peat was found to be a cheap and efficient alternative fuel. As well as use on domestic hearths, the peat can also be used for industrial purposes, such as fuel for power stations. On the Bord na Mona systems, after the peat has been drained and cut it is piled up beside the 3 ft (918mm) gauge railway lines, which are laid across the bogs. From here modern diesel locomotives haul the peat to factories where it is milled and compressed into briquettes for domestic fires, or to power stations where it is blown into the furnaces in the same way as pulverised fuel.

Wheat

There are several types of agricultural railways in North America. In the mid-western United States. Large grain elevators are used to store harvest products, usually corn or wheat. Many of these elevators are served by industrial switch engines which shunt the main line freight cars around as they are loaded from the elevators. There are similar operations that can be found in large grain terminals including those at Duluth, Minnesota and Buffalo, New York. Grain distributors, such as K. & L. Feeds in Franklin, Connecticut also operate their own locomotives and track.

Above: A scene on Sudan's Gezira light railway. This British-inspired system serves one of the largest cotton growing areas in the world. Here, one of the system's many Hunslet-built 600mm 0–8–0 diesels is seen in an exchange siding.

Left: One of the delightful 0–4–0 Fireless engines at Ludlow Jute Mill on the River Hooghly, upstream from Calcutta. Built by Orenstein & Koppel, the type of engine is a wise choice for industries where sparks from a conventional engine could wreak havoc.

MINERALS AND METALS

Below: This Dübbs A Class 4–8–2 Tank was built in Glasgow, Scotland in the 1890s. Formerly of Natal Government Railways it was pensioned off to goldfield service, and now operates at the East Daggafontein Gold Mine, Springs, in South Africa's Transvaal. Many Steam locomotives can still be found active on South Africa's gold fields.

South Africa (Gold Mine Railways)

In South Africa, gold mines were developed with railway networks, the country being one of the world's largest suppliers of gold. One of the more important gold mines was City Deep at Johannesburg which used six North British 4–8–4Ts. Trains operated 24 hours a day. The gold ore was hauled from the shafts to the mill from the two main shafts. From here the trains carried the ore to the junction with the main line at Jupiter station. Other South African mines that had their own rail networks included the Lorainew, at Allanridge, the President Brand and the President Steyn, the later two being at Welkom, in the Orange Free State. Like City Deep, all these systems used North British built eight-coupled tank locomotives.

Namibia (Diamond Mining Railways)

The diamond mining railways of Namibia were first set up by the Germans in the late 1890s. From the beginning they employed first generation electric locomotives, mostly 0–4–0 and Bo–Bo types built by Siemens of Germany. These trains conveyed rock and spoil from the diamond mines. After World War I, Namibia was ceded to South Africa under a League of Nations mandate and the De Beers Company took over responsibility for the diamond mines and that is still the case today, despite the recent independence of the country from South Africa.

Angola and the Congo (Cobalt, Manganese and Copper)

The Benguela Railway in Angola, which stretches from Lobito on the West Coast via Benguela to the Congo border at Luau, is 838 miles (1,348km) long. This railway, which was constructed between 1904 and 1929, represents one of the most important outlets of precious minerals from Central Africa bound for export. Until the Angolan Civil War in 1975, the Caminho Ferro de Benguela represented one of the most efficient railways in Africa. Owned by Tanganyka Concessions, a subsidary of the Belgian firm of Union Minier, after two decades of near abandonment, at the time of writing, there are moves afoot to rebuild the whole railway.

Jamaica (Bauxite Railway)

The bauxite railways of Jamaica were built to transport what is perhaps one of the most important sources of income produced by this Caribbean island. The railway network, which was set up through finance from both the USA and Britain, fed the standard gauge Jamaica National Railways with train loads of bauxite to be transported to seaports for export to all parts of the world. Since the closure of the national railway network in the mid-1980s, this industrial operation has been the only rail service of any kind on the island. Steam traction, which was largely American in origin, was superseded by American Bo–Bo and Co–Co diesels in the late 1960s.

India (Aluminium)

Renukut is the home to a hugely successful aluminium plant which has its own 5ft 6in (1,683mm) gauge system. This is used for drawing rakes of coal to fire the smelter. Such are the heavy loads needed to be hauled, that powerful, former Ghat banking locomotives are used to move the large quantities of bogie coal wagons.

Australia (Copper)

The wild, mineral-rich country of Tasmania possesses huge deposits of tin, lead, silver, gold, copper and iron ores. The terrain is far too difficult for road construction and so access to the deposits was generally achieved by tramways or railways. One of the earliest horse-worked tramways was constructed at the Mount Bischoff tin mine in 1878 but this was soon converted to a 3ft 6in (1071mm) gauge steam railway.

The Mount Lyell Mining & Railway Company built a torturous 21-mile (34km) long line connecting their copper mine with the coast. Going through lush rain forest, first alongside the Queen River and then through the King River Gorge, it included a 4½-mile (7km) long rack sections of 1 in 16 and 1 in 20. The copper and barytes from the mine were loaded on to shipping at Regatta Point. There were five 0–4–2T locomotives working on the Abt rack and pinion principle which hauled trains over this difficult route, the first of which went into service in 1896.

Left: A narrow gauge industrial diesel at the Awaso bauxite mine in Ghana.

Below: Loading bauxite from the hoppers onto Ghana Railways' main line wagons.

Right: A scene on the remarkable stone railway in Sumatra. This 600mm gauge Orenestein & Koppel 0–6–0 Well Tank, hauling a rake of stones that have been taken from a river bed, is bound for the crusher where the stones will be converted into track ballast for use on the Indonesian State Railways' main lines.

HIDDEN CORNERS OF INDUSTRY

Stone Hauling Railways of North America

Some of the earliest lines built in North America were for carrying stone. In 1826, the 3-mile (4.8km) long Granite Railway was built at Quincy, Massachusetts to haul stones to the site of the Bunker Hill monument. This line was not steam powered, but used animals to haul the stones. The Chester & Becket, also in Massachusetts, was used to haul stone down to Chester which was the location of stone cutting facilities and a connection with the main line. Other quarry lines were isolated from all other rail connections, and were used to move stones solely within the quarry facilities.

The Incredible Stone Railway of Sumatra

Interesting as they were, the New England railways pale into insignificance compared with the remarkable railway at Gunung Kataren. This 600mm gauge line was built to transport the smooth, flat stones, which had been manually retrieved from the bed of the fast flowing river. From the riverside the stones were conveyed up to a primitive stone crusher which stood next to the state railway's main line between Siantar and Tibingtinggi. Part of this fascinating line, which was used for the production of ballast, involved a cable-operated incline up which the wagons had to be hauled, one by one.

The Bass Brewery Railway

The brewery firm of Bass, Ratcliff & Gretton once operated a railway system that ranked as one of the most notable of its kind. In its prime the firm's locomotives worked over 16 miles (25.5km) of private lines that connected with the main line at Burton-on-Trent. At the Shobnall complex 8 miles (13km) of track served the maltings, cask-washing plant, experimental bottling stores and ale-loading stations. The area also included an extensive fan of sidings known as 'Klondyke' which had a storage capacity for 400 wagons. The connections and siding between the three main breweries absorbed a further 5 miles (8km) while there were another 3 miles (4.8km) of line at the Dixie Exchange Sidings and Stores.

The first part of the system was in operation by 1862 and, as the brewery expanded, so did the rail-

way, the last part being built in 1891. An interesting point about the system was that in many places it crossed public roads, making necessary its own signal boxes at the various crossings. In the 1920s the system was handling over 1,000 wagons a day. About one third of these were empties returned from the main line and the rest were involved in the inter-brewery traffic for the distribution of malt, barley, coal, etc.

Port Sunlight, England

A 2-mile (3.2km) long internal railway was built at the Port Sunlight refinery in 1910. The line connected the refinery and margarine works with both Bromborough Dock and Port Sunlight main line station. In 1913, nine passenger coaches were bought from North London Railway for transporting the company's employees to and from the main line station. As there was no platform, access to the coaches was by cinder ramps. The railway was operated by 0–6–0Ts built specially for the line by Andrew Barclay of Kilmarnock, Scotland.

Cadburys and Guinness

In the early 20th century the Cadbury Company built an extensive railway to serve their chocolate factory at Bournville, near Birmingham. This railway was used to bring in the cocoa beans and coal used in the manufacture of chocolate products. It also served to transport the finished products to the main line on the first stage of their journey to all parts of the world.

The Guinness Company constructed an extensive railway network of 5ft 3in (1,596mm) gauge and 1ft 10in (560mm) gauge to service their brewery in Dublin. This network, which ran in conjunction with barges on the River Liffey and the Irish main line railways was used to transport the finished product within Ireland and for export around the world.

Banana Railways

The American-owned International Fruit Packing Company constructed a large mileage of mostly 3ft gauge railways in Central America. These were used to transport fruit grown in these countries, especially bananas (hence the term 'Banana Republics').

Above: An Aveling Porter 0–4–0 tank with geared transmission. Built in 1906, this 'slow heavy hauler' worked at Richard Garrett's engineering works at Leiston in Suffolk, England.

9 the **railway's** **ROLE** in **Wartime**

FROM THE BEGINNING of the war the Confederacy was greatly in need of locomotives and rolling stock. As well as the North controlling two thirds of the nation's railroads, there was no locomotive building shop in the South and only one rolling mill, at Atlanta, that could make rails. President Lincoln saw early, the importance of the railroads, and one of his first orders on the outbreak of hostilities was to put them all under government control, with Andrew Carnegie as Superintendent in Charge. The South, however, did not recognise their importance and left them all in private hands.

The South Captures Union Locomotives and Rolling Stock

One of the Southerners who did see the strategic significance of the railroads was General Thomas Jackson who, in May 1861, devised a plan to relieve the Union of locomotives and rolling stock from the Baltimore & Ohio Railroad. In just two hours he captured 56 locomotives and 350 cars going both east and west between Point of Rocks and Martinsburg. These he ran along the 32-mile (51.5km) long branch line to Winchester from where they were removed by horses to the railway at Strasburg and so on to Richmond. While the loss of this, the largest capture of railroad equipment that would be made during the whole war, crippled the Baltimore & Ohio for many months, the gain to the scantily stocked Virginia railroads was invaluable.

Troops Arrive on the Battlefield by Train

At the first major battle at Manassas on 21 July 1861, in which Jackson received the sobriquet 'Stonewall', some of the Southern forces arrived by train, almost onto the battlefield itself. It is an interesting point that whereas the Union named battles after rivers, the Confederates named them after the nearest railroad depot – in this case Manassas Junction (on the Orange & Alexandria Railroad), through which the Bull Run river flowed.

Rail-Mounted Mortars

Both sides used flat railcars on which to mount heavy guns. One such was the Confederate 32 pounder rifled gun mounted on a railcar, which was protected from cannon shot by plates of iron through which a porthole for the gunner was pierced. This was used to good effect by the Confederate forces at Savage's Station on 29 June 1862. At the Siege of Petersburg, April 1865, General U. S. Grant brought into service the *Dictator*, a mortar gun that weighed 17,000 pounds and which could fire a 300 pound round shell five miles. Supposed to 'dictate' the peace, the gun was mounted on a flat car and moved to a 'Y' section of track from where it could fire in three directions.

Railroad Destruction

At the beginning of 1863 the South had only two rail lines of communication between their Western and Eastern forces. One was the coastal route to Savannah and thence westward, and the other by way of Chattanooga where it branched towards Memphis and Atlanta. On the Union's march from Atlanta to Savannah a 50-mile (80km) wide length of countryside, including the railroad, was 'Shermanised', leaving nothing but burning ruins.

It was not only the Union army who destroyed the railroads, they were also prone to frequent raids by the Confederates who destroyed bridges, tore up the tracks, burnt the sleepers and bent and twisted the rails in an effort to prevent the invading North from advancing.

The Locomotive Chase

A minor incident of the war, which has since been romanticised beyond belief, involved the capture at Big Shanty, Georgia, of the locomotive *General*. On 12 April 1862, at 6am 20 Union spies, led by James Andrews, hijacked the *General* while its crew was eating breakfast in the nearby Lacy Hotel. When they realised what had happened the crew rushed out and, commandeering a push-cart, gave chase. After eight hours and 87 miles (140km) the *General* ran out of wood and the chase ended near Ringold.

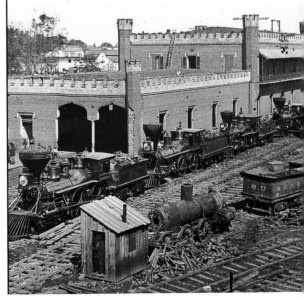

Below: During the Civil War Nashville was a very important railroad junction. This contemporary view shows an imposing line-up of typical US wood-burning locomotives of the 1850s outside the castellated railroad depot.

THE FRANCO—PRUSSIAN AND BOER WARS

Above: **An armoured Train constructed at the Cape Government Railway Works, Salt River, South Africa, for use by the Imperial troops.**

Right: **Norvals Bridge was in the front line of the fighting during the Boer War. It crossed the Orange River, which formed part of the border between British Cape Colony and the Boer controlled Orange Free State. A troop train is seen here crossing the bridge during a lull in the hostilities.**

The Franco—Prussian War 1870

After the American Civil War, the next major use of railways by the military came in 1870, with the outbreak of the Franco—Prussian War. The Prussians had already built a network of military railways that linked the state's main lines with strategic points on the system. Not only this, but the Prussian army had also evolved an embryo railway division, Die Eisenbahntruppen, which was both military and railway trained. During the war this planning paid off and helped the Prussian advance that led to their final victory.

Like the French, the Prussians used existing locomotives and rolling stock from state or private main line companies. The brevity of the war ensured that there was no time for any special military equipment to be built. The Prussian military engineers were well trained and able to build and re-build structures and equipment with a high degree of competence.

The French, on the other hand, were badly organised and had almost no co-ordination between the railway companies in the eastern border area and the military. This led to chaos, with stores and ordnance being stockpiled at Metz and Strasbourg. French irregulars did a great deal of damage to the Prussian advance by blowing up a number of troop and supply trains.

The Boer War 1899—1902

Shortly after the outbreak of the Boer War in 1899, it became apparent that good railway communications would be essential if the British were to secure a favourable outcome. An overall plan was formulated which provided a long-term policy towards the use of South Africa's existing railways as well as planning new military lines that were needed to further the war effort. Part of the policy involved setting up the Imperial Military Railways which

administered the Cape and Natal Government Railways during the war.

From early on, the Boer irregular forces played havoc with the rail network by blowing up bridges and destroying track. Although the British widely used armoured trains to try to protect the main arteries of communication, it was often to no avail, as the Boers blew up the track on their side of the train. Quite apart from the use of armoured trains and locomotives, mostly Class 7TH 4–8–0s and Class 4TH 4–6–0s, the British used large 4–8–2Ts built by Dübs of Glasgow. With the exception of some minor 2ft gauge lines in Cape Colony and Natal, most of the South African network was built to a standard gauge of 3ft 6in (1066mm).

The British also had, by way of the Cape Government Railways and the Imperial Military Railway, a through line from Cape Town to Bulawayo in Rhodesia which, for strategic reasons, had to be kept open. The only alternative was the 2ft gauge Beira Railway from the Mozambique coast to Rhodesia's border town of Umtali. Despite its small gauge the Beira Railway played a great part in moving troops and equipment to the Northern Front. Later, due to the volume of military traffic, it was rebuilt to the standard 3ft 6in gauge.

The railways in the Boer Orange Free State and the Transvaal, which had through connections to Portuguese East Africa (Mozambique), were also of standard gauge. One of the most important was a small system of lines in the Transvaal that ran from Johannesburg to Koomati Poort. As to locomotives, the Boers had German-built 0–6–4Ts and 0–4–0WTs that later became SAR standard classes. Like the British, the Boers used standard passenger and goods wagons, especially the standard African bogie drop-side trucks. After the end of fighting in 1902 all the Boer railways and equipment were taken over by the Imperial Military Railways.

Above: **Prussian troops say goodbye to their loved-ones before departing Berlin for Mayenne.**

Above: During World War I most of the waring nations used the railways. In this scene of 1917, a group of Japanese soldiers in Western Russia, pose by the side of a captured locomotive.

Right: During World War I, the British, to ease troop movements, laid a number of light railways in North West France. Here we see one such, laid by the Royal Engineers, conveying soldiers through a shell-shocked town.

THE FIRST PLANS FOR THE MODERN day use of railways by the military were formulated during the 1890s by the Germans who, under the Schliffern Plan, realised at an early stage the strategic value of railways in the theatre of war. As we have seen, during the Franco–Prussian War railways had proved, to a limited extent, to be useful in the advance of Prussian troops when invading France. The lessons from this, together with those learnt in the Crimea and during the American Civil War, were studied and digested by the German Imperial Government who formulated plans for the construction and storage of a large amount of military railway equipment in preparation for any future war in Europe or elsewhere.

In the years that led up to August 1914, the Great Powers formulated plans for war. These plans included logistics and the use of railways, both main line and military narrow gauge, mostly of 600mm, which was essential for fighting and winning the war. Railways had a profound effect on the outcome of the war and the shape of transport operations in the immediate post war period. Before the outbreak of war, the French, German, Austrian and Russian governments had built and stockpiled railway material for the construction of front line systems. The result of this was that in the months and years after August 1914 the Great Powers constructed over 1,000 miles (1,600km) of narrow gauge trench railways alone, from the Belgium to the Swiss border.

Field Railways

The military railways were made up of newly constructed 600mm gauge equipment, captured and adapted metre gauge rural light railways, and standard gauge railways truncated by war. The French had built narrow gauge Decauville systems at various locations. These lines served the fortified gun batteries in and around the forts at Verdun, the site of the 1915 siege.

The Germans constructed prefabricated field railways on site, some of this equipment having been supplied to the Austrians for use in the Balkans and the Dolomites. The Russians had a light network of 2ft 6in (762mm) gauge railways on the Baltic coast and a network of 600mm and metre gauge systems on the Russo–Turkish border.

The British, who first used military railways in the Crimea in 1854, were slow to realise the value of railways in war. However, for all that, soon after the outbreak of war, they ordered materials from specialist manufacturers such as the two firms of Hudson and Hunslet of Leeds.

The British constructed 1ft 11½in (629mm) gauge lines in Belgium, France, Egypt, Palestine and Salonica. In addition to the narrow gauge networks there were also a large number of standard gauge railways built by the military, both on the Western Front and other areas such as Salonica, Egypt and Palestine. In 1917 the Americans came into the war and with them, more equipment.

German Rolling Stock

The narrow gauge equipment, designed by the Great Powers, had similar features, with bogie wagons and locomotives of similar capacity.

THE FIRST WORLD WAR

The Germans used Orenstein & Koppel-built 0–4–0WTs and Krauss 0–8–0T Brigade types, while the British utilised Hunslet 4–6–0Ts, Baldwin 4–6–0Ts, Alco 2–6–2Ts, Hudson Barclay 0–6–0WTs and 0–4–0WTs. They also put into service Simplex, Crewe type, and Alco petrol locomotives.

THE FIRST WORLD WAR

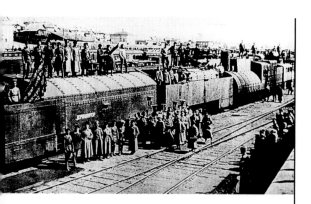

Above: After the 1917 October Revolution fighting still continued between the Communists and the White Russians. Here we see a Soviet armoured train at Kazan in 1918.

Right: Soviet sailors stand guard by a wrecked train in 1917.

The Allies' Rolling Stock

The British also used a variety of locomotives borrowed from main line railway companies together with War Department owned Great Central 2–8–0s designed by Robinson and a large number were built. The French used Fairlie type 0–4–4–0T articulated artillery locomotives were used on 600mm trench railways and fortified locations. They also used 'Haig'/'Joffre' type 0–6–0WTTs that were built in Britain and France for the French army.

The French also used captured locomotives, mostly 600mm German classes such as the Feld-bahn 0–8–0Ts which were acquired in large numbers during advances and tactical withdrawals.

The US troops had Alco 2–6–2Ts and petrol locomotives in use on 600mm trench railways. They also used Baldwin-built bogie petrol locomotives on the standard gauge feeder lines together with 'Pershing' 2–8–0 heavy freight locomotives newly built for use by the US Army as well as Baldwin 4–6–0s, 2–6–2STs and 0–6–0PTs.

The Belgian and British forces also used 0–6–0 tram locomotives on the Belgian Western Front while the Germans used standard G8 class 0–8–0 tender and P8 class 4–6–0s, together with captured engines on standard gauge lines that they controlled.

Moving Troops and Supplies

It was not only the Western Front that had a large mileage of narrow and standard gauge military railways. The use of railways to move troops and stores proved invaluable in other areas of the conflict. The British used a considerable amount of equipment in Egypt, Palestine and Salonica. This included GWR Armstrong 0–6–0 outside-framed, Dean 0–6–0 and LNWR DX class goods locomotives. The British built and operated a network of 2 ft gauge lines at Gallipoli, mostly horse- or mule-powered. They also acquired a considerable number of US-built Baldwin 4–6–0 tender locomotives used in Egypt and Palestine.

Middle East

Before the war the Germans had helped to build both the Hedjaz and the Baghdad–Basra railways. Ostensibly these were civilian lines but in reality they were military railways built under the cloak of advancing transportation in the Turkish Empire. On the Baghdad–Basra Railway the Germans supplied a large number of metre gauge locomotives of all wheel arrangements to met the needs of traffic.

For the Hedjaz Railway the Germans supplied Hartmann 2–8–0s, Jung 2–6–2Ts and Borsig 2–8–2 tender locomotives. The French later added a fleet of De Dion four-wheeled petrol railcars after taking over the Hedjaz lines in Syria at the end of the war. The use and value of the Hedjaz Railway to the German and Turkish war effort was cut short when Colonel T. E. Lawrence ('Lawrence of Arabia'), with his organised army of Bedouin guerrillas, destroyed the railway at various at strategic points, thus making the line almost unusable by the Turks.

The Balkans and Dolomites

The Austrians were supplied with German Feldbahn 600mm gauge equipment for use in the Balkans as well as U class 0–6–2 tanks and 0–8–0 tender locomotives built by Krauss of Linz. The Austrians were fighting on two fronts at this time. In the East they were holding the Russians on the Serbian border while, in the West, the Italians were being fought and held on the south–western border of the Dolomites. Italy claimed the area as part of its territory and here, the Austrians used light railways of 2ft 6in (762mm)gauge.

Post-War use of Military Railways

After the war, much of the equipment which had been built during the conflict was used for civilian use, thereby providing a form of relief to war-torn railways along the Western Front and elsewhere. The Palestine railways took over the American-built Baldwin 4–6–0 tender locomotives that had been used by the British in Egypt and Palestine. Some of the Austrian 600mm gauge lines and equipment that had been used in the Balkans remained in civilian service until the early 1960s.

Below: A Baldwin 4–6–0T at a factory in India, built for Britain's 600mm gauge line during World War I. This design formed part of the allied equipment of the 600mm gauge German Feldbahn 0–8–0T.

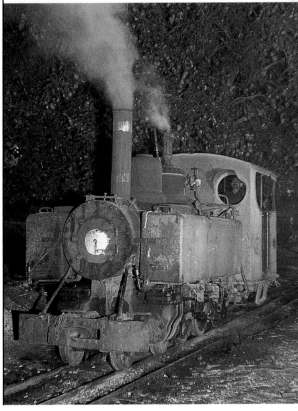

Above: A Greek Tank engine stands next to an AB Class, only one of which, in 1991, was still in full working order. Both these types were put to sterling service during World War II.

THE SECOND WORLD WAR

UNLIKE WORLD WAR I, which was fought mainly in trenches in Northern France, World War II was a mobile war, covering a large number of locations across the globe. Railways were, in many of these areas, an essential part of the war effort (on both sides of the conflict) and played their part in the final outcome.

Britain

At the outbreak of the war the British, apart from a small fleet of locomotives and rolling stock on the military railway at Longmoor, had little or no dedicated military railway equipment. The Longmoor Military Railway, on the South Downs, had been built by the Royal Engineers in 1903, and joined with the London & South Western Railway at each end. The southern connection was at Liss while the northern was at Bordon. Seeing the importance of the railways the government put the four main railway companies (the GWR, LMSR, LNER and SR) under central control. For the duration they were operated by 'The Railway Executive' with headquarters at the disused Down Street station, on London's Piccadilly Line.

The amount of equipment that had to be moved to keep the war effort going was enormous. For 1,000 bomber aircraft to take to the air on a mission, the railways had to move 650 tankers of fuel and 362 wagons of bombs. To enable this to happen, junctions were built between once competing lines to avoid unnecessary diversions and shunting movements. The locomotives used in the early war work included GWR Dean Goods 0–6–0s, LMS 0–6–0 diesel mechanical shunters and 'Jinty' 3F class 0–6–0Ts.

British Armoured Trains

During 1940, when invasion looked increasingly likely, the railway companies assembled 12 armoured trains for patrolling coastal lines as well as others that could possibly see activity from enemy troops. These armoured trains consisted of a locomotive in the middle with wagons fitted with guns, usually of World War I vintage on either end. One of these trains was on the 15in (380mm) gauge miniature railway that operated from Hythe to Dymchurch. By 1940, because of its coastal location, the area was under military control and locomotive No. 7 *Hercules*

and two bogie wagons were despatched to the Southern Railway works at Ashford to be converted into an armoured train complete with guns. The line, which in peace-time had been so popular with holiday-makers, often came under attack from enemy aircraft, pilots having great difficulty in differentiating between the miniature line and its bigger brothers!

British War Locomotives

In October 1939, R. A. Riddles, head of the LMS Mechanical & Electrical Department in Scotland, was appointed Director of Transportation Equipment at the Ministry of Supply. One of his first tasks was to provide for the British and French armies with an additional 10,000 covered wagons for use by French Railways.

Heavy duty freight locomotives were essential and 335 Stanier 8F class 2–8–0 were ordered by the Ministry of Supply for use in the Near East. The War Department also borrowed some LNER Class O4, ex–GCR/ROD (Railway Operating Division) 2–8–0s and three Southern 0–6–0DM shunters as well as setting up additional training facilities on the Shropshire & Montgomeryshire Light Railway and on the Melbourne branch of the LMS. Between 1943 and 1945, in an effort to save materials, the War Department produced the Austerity type 2–8–0s and 2–10–0s, over 1,000 of which were built. Because of their intended use overseas, the WDs, as they became affectionately known, were fitted with both Westinghouse air and vacuum brakes.

Evacuation

Britain's big cities, especially London, were prime targets for enemy bombs and the evacuation of children was considered essential. As early as 1938 the main line companies and London Transport began to establish a system for the evacuation of large numbers of children, between the ages of 3 and 13, from London, Liverpool, Manchester, Leeds and Glasgow to the country. When war was declared, the companies needed just 24 hours to mobilise staff and resources. Children were taken to stations to begin journeys to locations as far afield as Devon, South Wales and Norfolk. Such was the high number of children involved, that the largest company, the LMS, had to run as many as 1,400 special evacuation trains over a four-day period.

Below: **Built in 1925 by Captain Jack Howey the double-track 15 in miniature Hythe & Dymchurch Railway runs for several miles on a stretch of the Kent coast bordering on Romney Marsh. During World War II the trains were fitted with guns and used for home defense.**

THE SECOND WORLD WAR

Above: A scene from the making of the film *Yanks*.

Below: During World War II a number of Garrett type locomotives were 'enlisted'. These were emblazoned with the 'W D' (War Department) insignature.

American War Engines

The role of the American railroads during the war was phenomenal. Freight and passenger tonnages greatly exceeded pre-war figures and 1944 proved the busiest year. Thousands of GIs were moved by rail to and from the ports and between 1 December 1941 and 19 January 1942, more than 600,000 personnel were moved across the USA. America and its railroads had entered the war with a bang.

In November 1942, the US Army Transportation Corps arrived in Britain. This coincided with the urgent need for more locomotives and rolling stock in Britain and, as the war progressed, in both Europe and North Africa. As well as nearly 800 S160 class 2–8–0s from the USA that passed through Britain during the war, many others were shipped elsewhere.

During the war, some 22,000 wagon kits of seven basic types were shipped from the USA. Assembly lines were set up at the Longmoor and Melbourne military railways and by D-Day, some 7,000 wagons had been assembled in Britain. At the peak of activity a complete kit of parts could be put together in as little as 45 minutes.

Germany

Like Britain and the USA, Germany also used their railway network to transport men and supplies. Their most common locomotive was the Class 52 'Kriegslok' 2–10–0, or 'War Locomotive', of which some 6,500 were produced both for service at home and in occupied countries. These machines, which were built on the success of the Deutsche Reichsbahn Class 50, were constructed both in German factories and in occupied countries. Because of the numerous builders the engines, whilst built to the same basic design, were not identical. At the peak of production, over 400 locomotives were being constructed in a month. As the war progressed, these useful locomotives could be found in most occupied countries, including Russia, where the 5ft (1,524mm) gauge tracks had to be re-gauged to the standard 4ft 8½in (1,435mm) to accommodate them.

Tanks and Big Guns on Rails

The Germans also built large fleets of armoured vehicles. Resembling army tanks on railway wheels, apart from the prominent buffers, they performed the same tasks as their road-based counterparts being used mainly for protecting lines in Eastern Europe.

In 1942 and 1943, the German manufacturers Krupp, supplied 25 large rail-mounted guns to the Wehrmacht. Weighing 218 tonnes, these monsters could fire between eight and 15 rounds per hour. Two have survived. One is in the USA and the other is housed in the Musee Du Mur, near Calais. It still has its guns pointing towards England.

Left: The MacArthur 2–8–2 is one of the most celebrated war engines of all time. Introduced during World War II for the United States Transportation Corps' operations in the Far East, the type also saw service on the metre gauge networks of India, Burma, Malaya, Thailand and the Philippines.

Below: During World War II the Soviet railways were the main means of transportation over the vast distances encountered in that country. This typical railway depot scene shows a train waiting to depart.

10 railway
DISASTERS

MISHAPS AND MISDEMEANOURS

Mishaps

Although there had been minor mishaps, the first known passenger railway fatality occurred at the opening of the Liverpool & Manchester Railway, on 15 September 1830. At Parkside, the train hauled by *Rocket*, stopped to take on water and several of the passengers got out to stretch their legs. Unaware of the possible dangers, they were standing in the tracks chatting, when a locomotive, which was parading on the other line, came down amongst the gathering 'like lightning'. All rushed off the line except William Huskisson, Member of Parliament for Liverpool who, in the confusion, did not get off the line in time. Thus occurred the first fatal accident on Britain's railways.

Although few animals are large enough to derail a train some can, such as the buffalo and Indian elephant. There are a few recorded incidents of elephants attacking trains in India such as the night in 1869 when the peaceful encampment of a herd of 70 elephants was thrown into panic as a noisy, fire-emitting train came by on the nearby East Indian Railway. One bull elephant, fearing that it was going to attack his herd, charged the engine head-on, derailing the train and, in so doing, killed himself and the driver.

Then, in 1894, an elephant ran into a train in the Saranda jungle near Goilkera, about 220 miles (354km) from Calcutta. As a result, the engine and seven vehicles were derailed. Although there were no human injuries, the pachyderm was killed by the collision. Its skull was preserved and is now on display in India's National Railway Museum at New Delhi.

Collisions with animals have also occurred in Britain, such as in 1984, when a train travelling from Edinburgh to Glasgow hit a cow at Polmont. The train was travelling at 85mph (137kph) and despite the application of the emergency brake, the leading coach was catapulted up the left hand bank killing 13 passengers and seriously injuring another 13.

Sometimes accidents occur for inexplicable reasons such as that which happened in 1905 when the 'Twentieth Century Limited', running between New York and Chicago, crashed at Mentor. The points, which had been correctly set for the main line, had been reversed, nobody knew how or why, and the 60mph-train (96.5kph) turned into the siding and crashed into the freight shed. The resultant fire soon spread to the leading coaches killing many passengers.

Misdemeanours

In the early days of railways it was not uncommon for boilers to burst. This was usually due to safety valves being tampered with by the engine crew in an effort to achieve greater power. One such accident occurred on 10 November 1840 when Thomas Scaife and his fireman Joseph Rutherford, were killed when the boiler of their locomotive, *Eclipse*, exploded in Bromsgrove station. As this is at the foot of the steep Lickey Incline it is a matter of conjecture whether or not the valve had been 'adjusted' in an effort to take the gradient. Both were buried in the local churchyard; their graves being marked by headstones into which pictures of locomotives have been carved.

Another grave reminder of a railway accident is in Leicester's Welford Road cemetery where two headstones recall an event of 2 September 1898. The graves contain the mortal remains of Edward Meadows and William Joyce, the engine crew of the 6.45pm St Pancras to Manchester express. The train was not due to stop at Wellingborough and as it approached the station was travelling at about 70mph (113kph). On the station platform two boys were playing with a luggage trolley, suddenly it swung round and went over the edge and on to the track. Unable to stop the train struck the trolley, became derailed and, in spite of the efforts of Meadows, ploughed into the embankment. In the accident several carriages were wrecked with many injured and six, including Meadows and Joyce, killed.

Above: Amazingly there were no fatalities when this cattle train careered straight through Harcourt Street Station, Dublin, and crashed out of the end wall into Hatch Street.

Below: The graves of Thomas Scaife and Joseph Rutherford who died when the boiler of their locomotive, *Eclipse*, exploded in Bromsgrove Station, England, in 1840.

DERAILMENTS

Above: Engineers survey a derailed Jinty and box van.

A TRAIN CAN COME off the track for various reasons such as excessive speed, downright carelessness and, as mentioned, animals that have strayed on to the line. The first serious derailment occurred in 1842 on the Versailles line in France. Unable to escape from their locked coaches, 42 people were incinerated by the ensuing fire. As a result of this accident the French abandoned the practice of locking passengers into their coaches to prevent them from jumping out while the train was still in motion.

Carelessness

One of the most serious railway accidents on the East Indian Railway occurred at Bihta on 17 July 1937 when over 100 were killed when the Punjab–Howrah mail train was derailed during the monsoon season. Usually, the train was hauled by a 4–6–0, but on this occasion it was being worked by an XB class Pacific. Although the speed was restricted to 45mph (72kph) the driver, under orders from the company, attempted to keep to his schedule. The subsequent government enquiry found not only that the railway had been negligent, but also that the EIR had tampered with witnesses in an effort to evade responsibility.

Another accident that was caused by crew carelessness was that in Peru on Christmas morning 1954 when seven lives were lost and a 40-car freight train wrecked. The crew had neglected to test the brakes before leaving and had therefore not realised that the brake hose was not connected to the train. The train ran away, completely out of control down a 20-mile (32km) 1 in 50 grade before jumping the track. Although the locomotive's brakeshoes were worn right through, an inspection found that the car brakes had never been applied.

High Speed

Another cause of derailments is trains travelling at too high a speed for the track conditions. This is not just a form of careless, but of utter incompetence. A case in point occurred on 14 January 1985 near Awash, 118 miles east of Addis Ababa, Ethiopia. The Djibouti to Addis Ababa train was on the single track metre gauge line approaching the curved bridge at Awash too fast. It left the tracks causing some of its coaches to crash into the ravine below. This horrific accident left 392 dead and another 370 seriously injured.

Armagh

The most serious train derailment to occur in Great Britain was on 12 June 1889 when a special excursion train, 15 coaches in length and carrying 940 passengers, including a party of school children set off from Armagh for Warren Point, Ireland. The first three miles of the journey was a steep 1 in 75–82 climb to Dobbins Bridge Summit and for this section Thomas McGrath, an inexperienced driver, requested a pilot locomotive for assistance. However, this was refused and so he had to work the train himself without the help of an additional locomotive. As he expected, the train lost speed on the climb and within sight of the summit the locomotive finally stalled.

McGrath decided to split the train in order to take the first five coaches to the next station over the summit and then return for the other ten. However, once the rear ten were uncoupled the vacuum brake was released and the coaches began running backwards. While this was happening the regular train, which had left Armagh some ten minutes after the excursion, was beginning the climb. Within minutes the runaway coaches crashed into the on-coming train, the first three being completely shattered and thrown down the 40-foot (12m) embankment.

As a result of this accident within a year it became mandatory for all trains to be fitted with continuous automatic brakes. Had this been the case on 12 June there would not have been 80 lives lost and another 262 injured.

Above: A tale of two engines on the Sudan Railways line from Rabak to Khana with a Class 500 4–8–2 No. 541 passing the wreck of its sister engine No. 514. Seven overturned and half buried engines remain in Sudan.

BRIDGES AND VIADUCTS

WITH THE COMING of the railways stronger bridges than ever had to be built. Hitherto bridges only had to carry relative light weights but with the advent of the locomotive they were expected to carry many tons. It is, therefore, perhaps surprising that there were not more accidents due to bridge failure than there were. Most of the accidents that did occur were due to the builders' inexperience in using in adequate materials, such as timber and cast-iron, for building the structure.

The first serious railway accident due to bridge failure occurred on the night of 20 January 1846 when heavy rain washed away part of the timbered trestle bridge that carried the line between Tunbridge and Penshurst in Kent. The driver of the up night goods train did not see the damage and was killed as his engine fell through the hole. A year later, the cast-iron girder bridge over the River Dee between Chester and Saltney collapsed just as the 6.15pm Chester to Ruabon train was crossing. Although the engine managed to reach the other side, the rest of the train was not so lucky and fell with the girder, killing five and injuring another 16. It was this accident that first brought seriously into question the use of cast-iron for bridges.

The Tay Bridge Disaster

As awful as the above two accidents were, they were overshadowed by the Tay Bridge disaster. The bridge, at the time the longest in the world, was designed by Thomas Bouch in the assumption that it would have a solid rock foundation. However, the River Tay's bed was not as firm as he thought and after 14 brick piers had been constructed he decided to reduce the weight by using cast-iron columns.

On that fateful evening of Sunday, 28 December 1879, shortly after 7pm in a howling gale, the Dundee bound train went on to the bridge and into the history books. As it began its crossing three great sections of the bridge collapsed, taking the train and the 75 passengers and crew with it.

At the subsequent inquiry it was found that the three main causes of the accident were, the excessive speed (45mph–72kph) with which trains crossed the bridge (thereby loosening the girders); the use of cast-iron; and the inadequate foundations. It was, however, not until 1891 that the Board of Trade ordered that cast-iron bridges were no longer to be made and that in future wrought-iron and steel had to be used.

Viaducts

Viaducts, of necessity, are prone to the high winds which sometimes blow through the valleys that they cross. Although there are no recorded cases of an accident due to a viaduct collapsing, there was a near miss in the Bhore Ghat, India. In 1867, a new eight-arch viaduct was built and in spite of small cracks appearing overnight the authorities insisted that it was safe. However, just four days after it had been pronounced safe, and 30 minutes after a train had crossed it the whole structure collapsed.

Owencarrow Viaduct

The Owencarrow river valley is one of the most desolate and wind swept places in all of Ireland. It was here, on 30 January 1925, that the Burtonport train was blown off the 30ft (9m) high, 380-yard (347.5m) long viaduct. Two of the three coaches were relatively lucky – one coming to rest at a drunken angle half on and half off the viaduct, while the other rolled onto its side. The third, however, turned upside down and was suspended in mid-air. The roof was torn off and its occupants thrown into the valley below. As a result of this disaster a wind gauge was installed at nearby Dunfanaghy Road station and trains were prevented from crossing if the wind force was over 60mph (96.5kph).

Left: The wrecked three car electric train is seen here in the water where it came off the trestle bridge at Atlantic City on 28 October 1906. As can be seen there were no parapets on the bridge to break the fall.

Below: An official inspects the damage from the north end of the broken Tay Bridge.

HEAD-ON COLLISIONS

Above: Wreckage from the head-on collision at Abermule on 5 February, 1921.

Right: The curious position of the engines in the head-on collision near Ludhiana, India.

Below: Dowsing the embers of the Quintinshill disaster of 1915. Coaches were set alight by the coals of the overturned engine.

HEAD-ON COLLISIONS ARE CAUSED by two trains being on the same section of track, an eventuality that is invariably due to the carelessness of the signalmen or other station staff. Although in most countries it is against all rules and regulations for two engines to be on the same section of single line at the same time (unless they are coupled together as part of one train of course) human error does sometimes creep in with disastrous results.

In the American Mid-West, due to the vast distances, there were many single line tracks over the wide expanses of the prairies. An inherent peril on these lines was head-on collisions and because of the high momentum of the trains many of these 'cornfield meets' caused many fatalities.

Another country with wide open spaces and single track lines is Australia. On the steep mountain line which connects the steelworks at Port Kembla in New South Wales with Moss Vale, dieselisation improved running times and increased train loads but it brought a new problem. The slow, continuous grind up the mountainside, with no activity required by the driver and the continuous rumble of the motor behind him, was inclined to lull him off to sleep with the result that two head-on smashes occurred. This resulted in the introduction of 'vigilance controls' on locomotives which ensures that the driver reacts at frequent intervals and is thus kept alert, otherwise the train automatically comes to a standstill.

Quintinshill

The worst ever head-on accident in Britain was that at Quintinshill in Scotland on 22 May 1915 when a special troop train carrying a regiment of the 7th Royal Scots crashed into the local train from Carlisle that was standing on the line. Such was the force of the collision that the tender coupling on the local train broke and its coaches were shunted some 136 yards (124m). The heavy 4–6–0 locomotive was itself driven back 40 yards (36.5m) and came to rest with its tender across the down line. The 15-year old troop train coaches, with their wooden under frames, were smashed to pieces. To make matters worse the coals from the overturned engine ignited the gas that illuminated the coaches. To compound the situation, one minute later, the Euston to Glasgow express ploughed into the wreckage and in so doing ran down many of the survivors of the first collision.

Despite the efforts of the Carlisle fire brigade the fire blazed all day and night. As a result of this accident, which cost the lives of 224 and seriously injured another 242, the abolition of gas lighting was urged, as was the introduction of steel rolling stock.

Abermule

The collision at Abermule, on 26 January 1921, was caused by two trains being on the same line due to the combined carelessness of the station staff. A typical case of the left hand not knowing what the right hand was doing, each of the four staff on duty thought that one of the others had carried out the safety measures in operation. The Aberystwyth to Manchester express was approaching Abermule when the driver saw the 10.50am local train from Whitchurch to Abermule coming straight towards him. He pulled hard on the emergency brake, but the driver of the local did not seem to see the express, for at the moment of impact it was still belching smoke and steam. Although the smaller locomotive was damaged irreparably and both engine crew killed instantly, the coaches were only slightly damaged. The express engine had its boiler torn clean out of the frames and twisted through 180 degrees while the leading coaches were telescoped resulting in 15 passengers killed.

11 why **STEAM** Disappeared

STEAM WAS LABOUR INTENSIVE

ONE OF THE PRINCIPAL CRITICISMS levelled at the steam locomotive was that it was labour intensive. Not only were the driver and fireman essential for every journey, however short, but also huge numbers of ancillary staff were required throughout the railway system to deal with tasks such as coaling, watering, oiling-up and ash disposal.

Long before the driver and fireman took over an engine, steam would have had to have been raised and maintained. An average engine lit from cold needed at least four hours to reach its working pressure. This meant that it burned quite a large quantity of coal while doing no work at all. In 1952, a survey found that of the total amount of coal used by a Great Western 'Hall' class 4–6–0 locomotive, up to 22 per cent was consumed in non-productive work such as standing, manoeuvring, cleaning and building-up the fire.

Routine Maintenance

One of the most common aspects of the steam railway was the plethora of engine sheds throughout the entire system. These were where the locomotives had to go regularly for such basic servicing as mentioned above. Although a main line engine would often be in steam for a week or more, frequent boiler washouts were essential. This involved dropping the fire and emptying the boiler of water. After which came the back-breaking work of manually scraping off the deposits that had built up in the boiler shell and the tubes. This was done by inserting rods and high pressure jets of water through inspection holes to remove the scale that had become encrusted which, if left, would impair the engine's steaming capabilities. Internal dirt was a powerful deterrent to good performance and efficiency for, even when perfectly serviced, the build up of ashes or clinker in the firebed, ash in the pan, soot in the tubes and char in the smokebox all had an adverse effect on steam production .

Additionally, other routine maintenance, such as valves and pistons and other lubrication systems all meant that much more attention was needed with steam than with other forms of motive power. Even the apparently simple process of turning a steam engine, could involve one or two hours. Today's modern practice, in which trains can be driven from either end, renders the concept of turning, a thing of the past.

Dirty and Disagreeable Work

Quite apart from the diversity of labour, the nature of the work was, by the increasingly affluent 1950s, regarded as anti-social in its nature. This progressive disinclination to dirty and disagreeable work made it increasingly difficult to ensure a consistently high standard. This attitude was not confined to the richer nations for even Latin American countries had a bias against the steam engine. A typical example of the unacceptability of working on steam locomotives was eloquently summed up in 1982, by a report submitted to Brazil's Teresa Cristina Railway by Dr Jose Warmuth Teixeira. In the report he outlined the adverse conditions to which he believed steam locomotive crews were exposed. These included:

1. Trepidation. Such was the amount of concentration that was required that the crew's nerves were always at fever pitch.

2. Vibration. When an engine was run down, its vibrations became almost unbearable. In many cases the lunging about at the back end of the train so wearied the crew that they would lose time by slackening the speed to try to ease the situation.

3. Sound pollution. Leading to hearing loss.

4. Thermic overload. Making the crew extra-prone to infection.

5. Vicious positions. Causing bad backs in later life.

6. Coal dust. A prime cause of lung infection.

7. Excessive light from the firebox. This could affect eyesight.

Considering the large number of steam locomotive drivers who lived to a ripe old age, the validity of some of the above may, in practical terms, be doubtful.

Below: One of the USATC 0–6–0Ts, principle wartime design for military operations during World War II, takes water at Drama in northern Greece. Post-war dispersal sent these engines to many countries.

THE SUPERIORITY OF DIESEL AND ELECTRIC TRACTION

Above: One of the Midland Railway's 3-cylinder 4–4–0 compounds on the turntable at Derby locomotive shed. Forty-five of these engines were built as Midland Railway express passenger engines between 1901 and 1909. Building continued under the LMS.

Below: A line up of Midland Railway inside cylinder 0–6–0s in a typical roundhouse. The turntable, from which all roads radiate, is visible in the foreground.

Fuel

Unlike the steam locomotive, the diesel uses an easily transportable fuel, of unvarying quality which has no waste products to choke the operating circuit and, just as importantly, requires no disagreeable disposal after use. Another point is that a steam locomotive needs a full head of steam before reaching its maximum potential while neither diesel nor electric locomotives require a warm-up period, and as such give higher tractive efforts on gradients and during acceleration.

Heavy Fuel Movements

One of the biggest arguments against steam was that vast tonnages of coal had to be moved from one part of the country to another. On extensive railway systems there had to be many depots where coal was stored for locomotive use. Not only did these depots have to be maintained, with high staffing levels, but they also took up vast areas of land. The irony of this was, of course, that in order for coal to be available at these various depots, it had to be transported there by coal-burning trains. For obvious economic reasons these trains were some of the longest and heaviest on the entire network.

A point to remember is that not all coal generated the same calorific value and it was only coal from certain areas that was viable for railway use. In Britain, coal from South Wales was the best, it being 13 per cent more efficient than that mined in Yorkshire. It therefore follows that there were some areas of the country, even if they had coal mines, that had to 'import' coal from other areas. By the early 1950s, not only were supplies of high grade coal needed for steam locomotives becoming increasingly difficult to obtain but those that were of dubious calorific value. It was these shortages of suitable coal, coupled with the availability of cheap oil, that finally sounded the death knell for the steam locomotive. A report in 1952 estimated the all-in costs per mile, including capital charges, were of the order of 2s 2d (11 pence) for diesel as against 7s 3d (36 pence) per mile for steam. Another economic point in favour of the diesel is that it can remain continuously available for up to 90 per cent of its total time.

Socially Acceptable Work

One of the major factors which accelerated the change from steam to other forms of traction was the antisocial nature, real or imagined, of the work. As we have seen, steam locomotive drivers and firemen worked in very hard and dirty conditions, whereas diesel and electric locomotive drivers were almost white-collar, working in their relatively sanitised cabs.

The Environment

Compared with steam, diesel and electric trains are environmentally friendly. With no smoke and steam to pollute the atmosphere, both people and buildings benefit. The exhaust of steam engines contains acids that not only get into people's lungs, but also eats into the soft stonework of buildings. Younger readers may not appreciate just how dirty our inner cities became in the 19th and first half of the 20th

centuries. From the 1960s, massive programmes of cleaning buildings have beautified our urban centres beyond recognition. Buildings, that were once thought of as nondescript were found, after the removal of a century of grime, to be handsome relics of the past.

Electrification is the best answer when the density of movement is sufficient to justify the high one-off costs of installing the equipment and building power stations. It is more practical to take the 'generating stations' off the locomotives and build instead, fewer larger ones on the ground. Electric traction is therefore the method of choice in areas of high population, especially round big cities where commuter routes are prime candidates for such modernisation.

Above: 'The Sunday Stoker' at Tubarao on Brazil's metre gauge Teresa Cristina Railway. The man is one of a small team of steam-raisers who, in the early hours of Monday morning, flit from engine to engine to tend the fires and keep the boilers topped up with water in readiness for a new week's working.

India

As recently as 1990, India was regarded as second only to China as the 'Steam Country' of the world. In many ways the two countries complimented one another; China had 8,000 active engines which embraced only six classes while India had only a fraction as many but with a far greater variety of types. India also offers steam on four different track gauges. The situation in India, however, has changed vastly since then and by 1997, the nation's steam heritage had been decimated. While Indian Railways have been modernising progressively over many years, feelings against steam, both practically and emotively, have hardened. It is now extinct on the broad gauge and, while a pocket of activity survives on the metre gauge system, with both the erstwhile YP class Pacifics and YG class Mikados, these too will have become a memory by the turn of the century.

On the narrow gauge, the last steam line from Pulgaon to Arvi succumbed to diesel haulage during 1997, leaving only the 2ft (610mm) gauge Matheran and the famous Darjeeling lines, both of which are tourist orientated, surviving with steam. However, due to cost-cutting by the Indian government, the Darjeeling Himalayan 'toy' railway, is also in danger of closing. Completed in 1889, the railway, winds its way 50 miles (80km) from the plains of West Bengal up to Darjeeling (7,250ft (2,210m) above sea level). Today, its condition is lamentable – stations are falling apart, the track is in danger of subsidence and the carriages are covered in soot. The only hope for the railway is the Darjeeling Himalayan Railway Heritage Foundation which, together with friends and advisors in the UK, is hoping to save the line and transform it into an upmarket tourist attraction.

Any visitor who remembers the joys of Indian Railways a mere 20 years ago would find the position today interminably sad. Yet, a visit made at the beginning of 1997, revealed some incredible broad gauge rarities lingering on in industrial service, including a heavy 0–8–4 hump shunter of GIP origin and the last of the mighty XE class 2–8–2s. These were the only examples left in the world of large, classically styled British Mikados and, at 200 tons in weight, were the last big conventional British steam locomotives left in world service.

Apart from the exceptions such as these, the most interesting and active steam lingers on in the sugar field railways of the North. Here again, remarkable paradoxes occur, in that a nation now virtually devoid of active steam, should have the world's two oldest steam survivors left in service in the form of the metre gauge 0–4–0s *Mersey* and *Tweed*, both built by Sharp Stewart's Great Bridgewater Street Works in 1873. It is a sobering thought that when these veterans were exported from Liverpool Docks, Queen Victoria had another 28 years to rule the British Empire.

Pakistan

In neighbouring Pakistan, the emphasis is on the 5 ft 6 in (1,676mm) broad gauge. It is even more interesting in that here, locomotives date back to the British Engineering Standards Association (BESA) designs of the beginning of the 20th century, and take the form of classic inside cylinder 0–6–0s and 4–4–0s whose spiritual home lies in the soft English countryside of late Victorian Britain. That such veterans are still lingering on in territories of the former Empire, almost one century later, constitutes one of the most fascinating aspects of the contemporary steam scene.

Burma

With little more than derelict engines left in Bangladesh, it is to Burma, or Myamyar, one seeks further survivors of the Indian subcontinent. This country, which was virtually closed to foreigners for almost two decades, has a fine residue of classic British types. Although less than 50 engines are on the books, at least three classes are covered; all are Indian Railways' standard designs of the 1920s and classes YB/YC will, after the cessation of India's metre gauge YPs, be the world's last Pacific locomotive, so ending one of the most flamboyant types in the history of railways.

Above: A scene at the Hathua sugar mill in Bihar shows the world's oldest steam survivor in the form of *Mersey*, an 0–4–0 built by Sharp Stewart of Manchester in 1873. It is seen alongside one of the American-built 600mm 2–6–2Ts that saw military service in Europe during World War I.

Left: One of Pakistan Railway's inside cylinder 4–4–0s at the country junction of Malakwai in the Punjab. Typically British, these engines were exported to the Indian sub-continent under the BESA Standard locomotive programme, introduced in 1903.

WHERE STEAM LINGERS ON – CHINA

Above: A China railway QJ 2–10–2 rolls a heavy northbound freight from Dalian past Saddle Mountain on the approach to Anshan.

CHINA IS *THE* STEAM COUNTRY of the world. With approximately 5,000 steam engines in active service, a number greater than the rest of the world put together, it is both surprising and disappointing that they are comprised of only three types. As an interesting contrast, Burma has less than 50 active locomotives, but also has at least three different types. In the case of China, a communist state, this is because central planning and the absence of competing commercial sources, make standardisation of types both logical and easy.

The world's most numerous steam type is the Chinese QJ class 2–10–2. The lighter JS class Mikado is the nation's other principal main line type, while industry uses the ubiquitous SY class Mikado – basically a classic American 'light Mike' of pre-World War II. Another reason for this startling and unprecedented standardisation is that many of China's railways have been built since World War II and this, combined with the long years of war with the Japanese, decimated much of their indigenous stock. So once communist rule was established, it was easy to start afresh with standardised systems.

During the late 1970s, China achieved international fame by worldwide press and television coverage when it was pronounced that she was still building steam locomotives. Indeed, during the 1980s, there were times when one QJ was being produced daily at the Datong Locomotive Works, situated on the edge of Inner Mongolia. Today, not only has new building virtually ceased, but there has been a massive change in thinking. The central Think Tank's edict that steam should be perpetuated was frustrated when the nation's railway bureaux achieved autonomy, opted for modernisation and simply stopped buying Datong's products. This precipitated a massive swing against steam on environmental, practical and operational grounds, making the situation in China today similar to that in Britain during the 1960s, wherein steam was discredited and every effort made to eradicate it from the nation's railways. Against this all-pervading idea, the historic locomotive building works at Tangshan are, at the time of writing, still building around one SY class 2–8–2 a month for industry – principally coal mining concerns. By the end of 1997 a total of 1,800 SYs had been built.

The Chinese are prepared to build new steam locomotives either for state railway use or tourist lines and Tangshan Works has already built a batch of Mikados for Vietnam and has also supplied some SYs for use on preserved railways in the USA.

If there is a bright spot on the Chinese steam scene it will be with those provincial lines which do not form part of the national state system. In general, these railways, built with local finance, will not be able to afford diesel, and certainly not electrification, and are likely to retain steam long after it has vanished from the state system. These provincial lines, along with an ever-dwindling number of industrial environments such as coal, iron, stone, forestry and manufacturing plants, will be found with steam for many years to come. In the case of the narrow gauge forestry lines, which are worked by standard 0–8–0s of both European and Chinese origin, some engines were also being built during the 1980s, but it is believed that this is now finished. It certainly seems that some steam locomotives will survive as far ahead as 2015, if any estimate of such matters has credibility.

Whilst this is both heartening and exciting, and will easily give the steam locomotive more than two centuries as a motive force, the spectacle of busy steam main lines with a variety of trains passing in an exciting non-ending procession as part of the nation's daily life had disappeared into oblivion from China Railways by 1995.

North Korea

In neighbouring North Korea some steam survives on non-electrified lines and in part on shunting duties. A wide variety of locomotives are believed to exist, not all working, and amongst well-known types recorded in this extremely difficult land to visit are USATC S160 class 2–8–0s and 0–6–0Ts and ex China Railways JF and JF6 Mikados. With the various problems the nation faces in the late 1990s, steam is likely to survive.

Left: A China Railways standard QJ Class 2–10–2 makes a laboured start at Sankong yard in Harbin with a south-bound freight.

Below: Building the world's last steam locomotives at Tangshan with the boiler shell for a new SY Class 2–8–2 industrial Mikado.

WHERE STEAM LINGERS ON – SOUTH EAST ASIA

Right: Dragon No. 6 on the Hawaii Philippine company's 3ft 6in (1,066mm) gauge network on the Philippine island of Negros. The engine was built by Baldwin's in 1920 and is seen here as an oil-burner, complete with stove-pipe chimney. Once enough bagasse – sugar cane waste – has been amassed, the engine will be converted to burn this and her traditional cabbage-stack spark-arresting chimney will be refitted.

Below: The last steam locomotive exported from Britain was this delightful Hunslet 0–4–0ST, which left Hunslet's works in Leeds in 1971. She survives at the Trangil sugar mill in Java.

Java

The most fascinating country to retain steam traction is Indonesia and in particular Java, which, for its size, had until the late 1970s, one of the most remarkably antiquated and varied locomotive fleets in the world. Although the diversity of the main lines has gone, it survives in abundance on the island's sugar plantations, where an array of multi-hued veterans can still be found, both at work and in moribund form. Java was once part of the Dutch East Indies and this is reflected in the vast majority of European locomotives, particularly from Holland and Germany, the latter represented in particular by Orenstein & Koppel. This Indonesian enclave is to European steam as Cuba is to American.

These steam-worked systems are operated by locomotives which have paid for themselves many times over, and run on bagasse, the dried and baled-up natural waste product of sugar cane processing which, albeit low in calorific value, is ostensibly free. Although many of the engines have spark arresting chimneys their effectiveness, especially with age, is questionable and it is a familiar sight to see shrouds of bagasse, still flaming, getting sucked off the firebed and flung into the atmosphere with great velocity, sometimes causing spectacular line fires. At times these engines resemble active volcanoes on the move. Although steam is declining rapidly in Java there is still much to see, including such delights as *Salak*, an 0–8–0 tank, built by O & K in 1910. Named after an extinct volcano, *Salak* is the world's last jack-shaft-driven steam locomotive. She is the finest hauling engine in Java, her slow, even torque being ideal for working over the omnipresent quagmires.

Sumatra

On the neighbouring island of Sumatra, the last vestiges of the steam age are ending on the palm oil plantations, where engines fired on nutshells – again the waste processes of the palm oil processing – operate deep into the plantations to convey the heavy fruit to the factories.

Philippines

Little steam survives in the Philippines, and that which does is centred on the island of Negros, where a wonderful network of sugar plantation lines have existed. Notable systems are the Hawaiian Philippine Sugar Company's magnificent 3ft gauge network which has seven active Baldwins known as 'Dragons'. Sadly, all vestiges of the legendary Insular Lumber Company have largely disappeared, but some of their classic American Shays and Mallets exist amid the over-growing vegetation. At Hawaiian Philippine the engines burn bagasse for the bulk of the season but are oil fired during the initial weeks, until sufficient supplies of bagasse have been accumulated.

Vietnam

South East Asia's other steam bright spot is Vietnam, where steam survives both in main line and industrial service. Although there are few locomotives in daily service, Mikados are active both on the metre gauge and standard gauge lines. Interestingly, steam is banned from Hanoi during daylight because of over-congested roads which pour traffic over the many level crossings. However, steam does work the main line to the south of here. In the steel works at Luuxa, which also operates standard gauge lines, metre gauge 2–6–2s and 0–6–0s are used for shunting. All steam is coal fired.

Vietnam Railways are crippled by bureaucracy, low wages, lack of foreign exchange and this, combined with the inevitable effects of the war during which the railways were extensively damaged, should ensure steam survival for some time. It is significant in being one the last areas of the world to have French derivative locomotives, a school which is all but extinct. The standard gauge 2-8-2s are of the China Railways JF type and are particularly valuable since they are classic American Mikados, which are on the verge of extinction in China.

WHERE STEAM LINGERS ON – AFRICA AND LATIN AMERICA

Africa

As the vast majority of African railways were built, or inspired, under European colonial rule it is not surprising that almost all the locomotives and rolling stock were imported, mostly from Britain, due to the country's colonial pre-eminence. The industries of South Africa made this country the continent's greatest steam user and, until only recently, one of the highlights of the world's 'steam scene'. However, the running down of steam and, to a lesser extent, the railway itself, has destroyed the rich diversity that once existed here. Today, only a handful of engines survive centred on gold mining and collieries.

In neighbouring Rhodesia, until recently known as the 'Land of the Garratt' as 90 per cent of its steam fleet was of this type, steam has largely been put aside in favour of dieselisation, although a handful of British-built Garratts from Manchester still survive on shunting and tripping duties around Bulawayo. To the East, Mozambique sees limited steam use, although sadly the world's last Atlantics now lie moribund.

No steam now survives in Ghana, the one-time perfect example of a British colonial railway and, doubly sadly, despite an appeal from the former mother country that some of the heritage be preserved, all aspects of the steam age have now been obliterated.

In the north east of the continent steam survives in two countries. The principal one is Sudan, which has battled bravely to maintain its excellent railway system along with some of the blue liveried British-built steam engines that work on it. Whilst, to the north in Eritrea, former railway employees, some in their 60s and 70s, are struggling to rehabilitate their main line railway, from Massawa to Asmara and Agordat, which was closed in 1974, and has suffered years of war damage. As and when the railway reopens it is likely to bring back 0–4–4–0 Mallet tanks built by Ansaldo of Italy in the 1930s. The exciting thing about this is that the rehabilitation of this railway will constitute a return to steam from an otherwise steamless country.

Latin America

Latin America, which once had some of the most exotic steam railways in the world, is like Africa, a dim shadow of its former self. The bright spot is Paraguay which operates the last all-steam main line in the world running from the capital, Ascunión, to Encarnación almost on the Argentinean border. This incredible railway was slowly coming back to life in 1997, following a cessation of traffic. Some of the Edwardian wood-burning Moguls, built by North British of Glasgow, remain in service. The railway's main works are set in the country village of Sapucay and are like a working museum, and arguably, the steam sight of the world with all plant steam-driven thorough belts in classic 19th century fashion. In contrast, nearby Uruguay has lost its once superb stud of pure British locomotives due to the running down of the nation's railways in favour of roads. The main casualties from Uruguay are the world's last 4–4–4Ts built by the Vulcan Foundry of Newton-le-Willows, England in 1915.

In Argentina little remains, although the 750mm Henschel 2–8–2s survive on the Esquel branch. Argentina's other 750mm gauge railway is in the far south running from Rio Gallegos to Rio Turbio with its Mitsubishi-built coal-carrying 2–10–2s and is in the process of being dieselised. The industrial railways of Brazil have proved a treasure house of discovery in recent years, but few are believed to operate steam now.

One other Latin American bright spot is Bolivia where some former Argentinean General Belgrano Line metre gauge 2–8–2s and 4–6–0s have made an unexpected return to steam working, especially for shunting at Guaracachi and possible use on the branch line to Yapacani.

Above: A scene on the Kosti to Khana line in Sudan as a blue-liveried, oil-fired North British-built 500 Class 4–8–2 overtakes a plodding Donkey cart.

Left: Large American-designed locomotives arrived in South Africa with the Big Ball 4–8–2s. Classified 15CA, one of the giants storms out of Panpoort on the line between Pretoria and Witbank.

Above: A Baldwin-built 2–8–0 of 1912 heads a rake of sugar cane to the Rafael Freyre sugar mill in Cuba's Holguin Province. The curiously shaped mountain in the background was one of Columbus's landmarks when he discovered Cuba in 1492.

Right: Baldwin-built Mogul No. 1604 of 1920 at Boris Luis Santa Coloma sugar mill at Robles flat crossing with a typical American-style signal box on stilts.

WHERE STEAM LINGERS ON – CUBA

CUBA, A COUNTRY APPROXIMATELY the size of Florida, will go down in railway history as being the last bastion of classic American steam power on Earth. This makes the island immensely important to railway historians and enthusiasts worldwide, as the American school of design was a corner-stone of world locomotive evolution. Thinking of American steam motive power in three basic phases; early beginnings, the middle years and the evolution of super power, Cuba's roster comes very much from the middle period. Nothing is older than 1878, and nothing more powerful than a beefy 2–8–2.

Cuba, following Castro's revolution of 1959 and the subsequent cessation of all trade with the USA, is unique in being frozen in time. Had the revolution not occurred, American commercial interests – which were rampant throughout all aspects of Cuban life – would have quickly ensured dieselisation. Devoid of these commercial interests, Cuba's agricultural economy, under a communist regime, inevitably had to maintain what technology it had. The prohibition period style American cars that ply the streets of Cuba's towns are another elegant result of this.

Although most of Cuba's locomotives were built specifically for the island, some are actually ex-American railroads pensioned off to Cuba for a further lease of active life. The Cuban roster reads like a Who's Who of the great American foundries with engines from such legendary names as: Alco, Baldwin, Davenport, H. K. Porter, Rogers and the Vulcan Iron Works. Locomotive types range from 0–4–0 and 0–6–0 saddle tanks to 2–6–0 Moguls, 2–6–2 Prairies, and 2–8–0s. A few 10-wheelers (4–6–0) can also be found along with the occasional 2–4–2T, 0–4–4T and several rare fireless engines.

Due to the fascinating variety of gauges, which include such rarities as 2ft 3in (686mm), 2ft 10in (864mm) and 3ft (914mm), as well as 2ft (610mm), 2ft 6in (762mm) and standard, few of the systems join. The exceptions are some of the standard gauge networks which link-in to the state railway main lines. These enable the sugar mill trains to run – often for considerable distances of 15 miles and more – as 'main line' trains where the distances from the cane fields to the factory necessitates through running.

Another example of extensive line working over the state system is the Fructuosa Rodriguez sugar mill which undertakes round trips of 37 miles (60km). From the mill they run to Limonar to connect with the state system, reversing at Guanabana and continuing to Cidra, where the trains 'disappear' into the cane fields to serve various remote loading points.

Even in Cuba the steam paradise is under threat and there has been a steady flow of Russian-built diesels for both standard and narrow gauges. Russian aid placed Cuba as the most socially developed society in the whole of Latin America. But the foreign reserves to buy new technology are limited and economic problems remain. the foreign reserves to buy new technology, with all the economic problems which front Cuba today, is impossible.

Cuban engineers are highly practised in the art of 'make do and mend' and there is every good reason that steam will remain active, albeit in ever-dwindling numbers for some years to come and that, less than 100 miles (161km) from the mainland, American engines will continue in full bloodied activity some half a century after their forebears vanished from the American landscape.

For the railway enthusiast a visit to Cuba is a never-to-be-forgotten experience. The country has all the makings of a paradise island; the world's most perfect climate, the most beautiful beaches, an enduring history, a people blessed with enormous charm, the world's finest cigars and classic American steam running like nowhere else on Earth, with sights and sounds recalling the USA of almost a century ago.

Below: A Baldwin 2–8–0 No. 1661 of 1920s-vintage belongs to Cuba's George Washington mill and is basking amid the sugar plantation at twilight. Note the yellow caboose, which forms an essential part of the train when running over Cuban State Railway main lines.

RAILWAY PRESERVATION in Britain began when the South Kensington Museum of Science and the Pure and Applied Arts (better known today as the Science Museum) acquired the famous *Rocket* locomotive in 1862. Over the next 60 years, various other engines were preserved by various companies, but it was not until after World War I that private enthusiasts decided that they too had a part to play.

Gladstone

In 1927 the first private action by enthusiasts was made when the Stephenson Locomotive Society bought *Gladstone*, one of Stroudley's famous 0–4–2 express locomotives of the former London, Brighton & South Coast Railway, from the Southern Railway. A year later the engine was placed on loan in the LNER's railway museum at York, where it still resides in today's National Railway Museum.

The Talyllyn and Ffestiniog Railways

Many years were to elapse, however, before the first railway was acquired by a preservation group. In October 1950, under the initiative of L. T. C. Rolt, a leading writer on transport affairs, a group of railway enthusiasts met in Birmingham to consider proposals for preserving the seven-mile (11km) long narrow gauge Talyllyn line. Enthusiasts soon formed what was to be the world's first railway preservation society and after many years of hard work by volunteers rebuilt the line along its entire length. In 1976, the line was also opened to passengers from Abergynolwyn, the original terminus, to the foot of the incline at Nant Gwernol.

The success of this project had inspired others and thoughts became centred on the derelict Ffestiniog Railway which ran from the slate quarries of Blaenau Ffestiniog to Porthmadog. Opened in 1836 this, the oldest public narrow gauge railway in the world, had been closed in 1946. In 1951, the newly formed Ffestiniog organization set about rebuilding the section from Porthmadog Harbour station to Boston Lodge, just over a mile away (1.6km), which was re-opened in 1955. It was not, however, until 1982 that the terminus at Blaenau Ffestiniog was reached, a feat of engineering which involved diverting the railway around a reservoir that had been built over part of the original trackbed. A new fea-ture was the spiral that was built in 1977 at Dduallt to enable the line to gain the necessary height to run alongside the reservoir.

The Bluebell Railway

In 1958 the standard gauge line from East Grinstead to Lewes, Sussex was closed. In 1959, a group of four student railway enthusiasts from the area, who had tried unsuccessfully to get BR to re-open the line, formed a society to run a section as a steam operated railway. The result was the first railway preservation society in the world intent on running a standard gauge passenger line. Known as the Bluebell Railway, so called after the abundance of spring flowers in the area, the first section, from Sheffield Park to Bluebell Halt, just outside the British Railways station at Horsted Keynes, opened in 1960. Although set up at a time when rolling stock and locomotives could be obtained direct from BR and put straight into service, the Bluebell has not been content to sit back and is currently re-opening the line in stages through to East Grinstead where a connection will be made with the national network.

Flying Scotsman

In the 1960s, with the British Railways' steam fleet fast becoming decimated, groups of enthusiasts and companies began to purchase locomotives for preservation. Undoubtedly the most famous locomotive purchased at this time was *Flying Scotsman*, acquired by Alan Pegler in January 1963. Originally one of Gresley's A1 Pacifics of 1923 it had subsequently been modified to Class A3 form. After purchase, the locomotive was restored to its appearance of pre-war days in LNER apple green livery and has since become the world's most travelled locomotive with visits to North America and Australia.

Above: A scene from England's preserved Bluebell Railway.

Below: An excellent example of a preserved Southampton & Chatham Railway C Class 0–6–0 locomotive, designed by Wainwright and built in the first decade of the twentieth century.

EARLY PRESERVATION IN AMERICA

AMERICAN RAILWAY PRESERVATION roughly mirrors the rise and decline of railroad operations in the United States. The first equipment preserved were antiques from the earliest days of railroading. Later, as various aspects of railroading began to vanish, railway preservationists began to collect and preserve appropriate equipment, structures, right-of-ways and literature.

The Baltimore & Ohio Railroad

The earliest American railroad was also the first to initiate railway preservation in the United States. The Baltimore & Ohio Railroad, chartered in 1827 to operate from Baltimore, Maryland, to the Ohio River, began operating steam-powered trains in the early 1830s. From the beginning, the B&O established a tradition of promoting its railroad to the public and this tradition evolved into the first American railroad preservation effort. During the 1880s and 1890s the railroad gathered a collection of historic railroad equipment that it displayed at railroad fairs and expositions.

In 1927 the B&O, to commemorate its first 100 years, sponsored the 'Fair of the Iron Horse'. A few years later the company's plans for a railroad museum based on its historical collection was delayed by the Great Depression and then World War II. The museum, based at its Mount Clare workshops in Baltimore, finally opened in 1953. Today, this museum, although no longer affiliated with the railroad, houses one of the best collections of preserved railroad equipment in the United States, including a 'Grasshopper' engine, the *Tom Thumb* replica, and Central Railroad of New Jersey's No. 1000 – the first commercially successful diesel-electric locomotive.

Private Preservation

In the 1920s the first enthusiast railroad preservation groups, such as the Railway & Locomotive Historical Society were formed, and set the foundation for early preservation efforts. During the 1930s American railway systems began to decline and lines, particularly interurban electric routes, were abandoned.

Three of the earliest museum efforts were aimed at preserving the electric railway tradition in New England. The Seashore Trolley Museum in Kennebunkport, Maine, the Warehouse Point Trolley Museum (now the Connecticut Trolley Museum) near Hartford, Connecticut, and the Branford Electric Railway (now the Shoreline Trolley Museum) east of New Haven, Connecticut all had their start before US involvement in World War II. However, the museum movement did not really get going until several years after the war.

In the 1950s and 1960s, as the last steam locomotives were being retired in favour of diesel-electric power, and long distance passenger services were in decline, renewed interest in railway preservation led to many new museum efforts. In Wisconsin, the Mid-Continent Railway Museum gathered a collection of Mid-Western cars and locomotives, including a nationally significant selection of wooden railway cars. The St Louis Museum of Transportation saved a number of important locomotives and today has one of the best representative collections in the nation. In Southern California, the Orange Empire Museum preserved railroad and streetcar equipment indigenous to that region, including some of Pacific Electric's famous 'Red Cars'.

Perhaps two of the most authentic examples of railway preservation in the United States are the East Broad Top Railroad, in central Pennsylvania, and the Cumbres & Toltec Scenic Railroad, which runs along the New Mexico and Colorado border. Not only have these two narrow gauge lines saved the locomotives and cars, they have also preserved the structures as well as the railroads' original operating environment.

Most preservation was the work of conscientious enthusiasts with limited resources and, along with privately funded museums, several history-conscious lines set aside significant equipment for preservation, notably the Pennsylvania, Santa Fe and Union Pacific railroads. There was, however, no national plan for preservation and many lines were unsympathetic towards saving historically important equipment, scrapping entire classes of locomotives and cars. As a result there are no examples of famous locomotives such as a New York Central Hudson type.

Left: A Baldwin 4–4–0 American type, preserved on the Old Tucson–Reno Steam Railway.

Below: Tom Thumb, currently housed in the Mount Clare workshops of the Baltimore & Ohio Railroad.

ENGINES ON PLINTHS

Below: The amazingly successful E series 0–10–0s, of which some 14,000 were built in slightly varying forms, was one of the most numerous steam class in world history.

IT WOULD APPEAR THAT all countries that have, or have had, railways commemorate the good service engines have given to the community by placing retired machines on plinths. Why should this be? Perhaps it is because the steam locomotive had the semblance of a well-loved person or animal – it ate (coal and water) and it breathed (smoke and steam), so, like worthy people who are memorialised after death, it was placed on a plinth in a place of honour.

What Kinds of Locomotive are Placed on a Plinth?

Mostly they are steam, but a number of electrics and internal combustion powered machines are also to be found at industrial plants. The types range from powerful main line locomotives to diminutive narrow gauge engines. For locomotives that have been in passenger service, there appears to be a preference for the little branch line engine. A mem-

ory that probably brought to the minds of those proposing to have an engine placed on a plinth, of travel to school or market in more relaxed times.

Others have great historical significance such as *Invicta* that ran successfully for many years on the Canterbury & Whitstable Railway in south-east England. For many years this locomotive stood in a public park whilst others, like *Tiny*, built by Sara & Co. of Plymouth in 1868 for the 7ft (2134mm) gauge South Devon Railway, stood on the platform at Newton Abbot station.

Where Can Engines on Plinths be Found?

Public parks sometimes have engines that, when stripped of moveable small parts, are provided as a feature for children's play. These can be far removed from a railway and, sadly, are often allowed to deteriorate and become dangerous to the public, leading to their ultimate removal and possible scrapping.

In the case of railway stations, engines are sometimes removed when the station is modernised, but usually locomotives placed on a plinth on railway premises, including at the lineside or at manufacturers' works, are well maintained. This can also be true of industrial sites – at least while the management that installed the machines remains responsible. A fine example of a locomotive readily accessible to the public is the German Class 01 Pacific in a grassed open space close to Brunswick (Braunschweig) station in Germany. Hungary is a particularly good country for plinthed locomotives. A diminutive 760mm gauge Class 490 tank engine has pride of place on the platform of Huvosvolgy station on the training railway near Budapest where children learn the skills to enable them to join the state railway. A streamlined 2–4–4T stands at Puspokladany, a neat 2–4–2T at Cegled and a Class 40 electric can be seen outside Budapest Keleti Pu.

Plinthed Engines Returned to Traffic

The incidence of engines being restored to working order following display on a plinth is quite rare. One example is *Licaon* that was placed on a plinth with two other locomotives just east of Linz station in Austria. It was restored in 1986 for the

150th anniversary of Austrian railways and has subsequently made guest appearances elsewhere outside Austria. Another example is Southern Pacific's famous 'Daylight' streamlined Northern type, No. 4449 which resided in a park in Portland, Oregon for nearly two decades before it was restored to service in the mid-1970s for work on the American Freedom Train.

In Ireland the Great Southern Railway Preservation Society is restoring a Class QS, built by Neilson Reid in 1900, and which stood on a plinth for 20 years in Dundalk.

The best example of a once statically displayed locomotive returning to service must be the National Railway Museum's LMS 'Duchess' class Pacific, No. 46229 *Duchess of Hamilton*. It has seen extensive operation on the main line in recent years but had previously spent many years standing in the open air at a holiday camp in Somerset.

So far as the writer is aware, there is no comprehensive published record of engines on plinths around the world. Various specialist societies have records and authors sometimes include details of preserved locomotives in lists in their books indicating that they are placed on a plinth and where they are to be found.

Above: As reward for years of faithful service this Spanish 0–4–T is retired to bask in the Andalusian sun.

Below: Avonside, an 0–6–0 Saddle Tank was the last steam locomotive to work in Britain. It is now relegated to guarding the entrance to Jose K Holt Gordon's scrapyard in Bolton, Lancashire.

THE WORLD'S GREAT RAILWAY COLLECTIONS

Europe

Although there had been many small local museums in Britain, the country's National Railway Museum at York did not open until 1975. This magnificent museum, which is being constantly improved, attracts many visitors (over 400,000 in 1996) who come to see every aspect of the railway age, from station signs to fully working locomotives. The NRM owns far more than it can show and as such allows some of its exhibits to be used by various operating railways and museums all over the country. Most European countries have their own national railway museums that display examples peculiar to that country. Opened in 1899, Germany's national museum in Nuremberg has the distinction of being one of the oldest, if not *the* oldest, railway museum in the world. The present building was opened in 1925 and expanded in 1984 when a new exhibition hall was opened. The French national museum, at Mulhouse, opened in 1976. Here, however, the emphasis is on locomotives and rolling stock with little to illustrate the impact of railways on French society or the economy. Switzerland's famous museum in Lucerne, which opened in 1959, is one of the most 'user-friendly' railway museums in Europe, inasmuch as all descriptions are in the four major European languages – French, German, Italian and English. This museum houses one of Europe's oldest working locomotives, *Genf*, built by Emil Kessler of Esslingen in 1859. Poland's first railway museum, established in 1928, shared the fate of the majority of that country's cultural institutions which were plundered and burned by the Nazis. The present museum, housed in Warsaw's Gtowna station, was established in 1972. Although very few of the locomotives on show have been renovated, they reflect the rich legacy of Austrian and Prussian designs, the most dramatic exhibit being a Pm3 streamlined German O3.10 Pacific, one of a batch received in reparations after World War II.

Right: Vienna has one of the most exciting technological museums in Europe. Here is a general view of the transport hall.

Below: The Adler, here on show in Switzerland's premier railway museum in Lucerne.

North America

The United States does not have a national railway museum, although in recent years the federal government has provided funding for projects such as Steamtown in Scranton, Pennsylvania. State funding predates national funding – the Railroad Musuem of Pennsylvania had its beginings in the mid-1970s, and the California State Railroad Museum opened in 1981. Other state sponsored railroad museums include those in Nevada and Pennsylvania – states where the landscape was greatly altered by the railroad. In general these state museums have been largely more effective than national efforts, that in California being the most visited railroad museum in North America. North of the border there is the Canadian Railway Museum in Montreal.

India

Outside Europe and North America the world's finest railway museum must be India's Rail Transport Museum, at Chanakypuri, New Delhi, which was opened in 1977. The first of its kind in the country, it covers an area of over ten acres. As well as the enclosed galleries there are also open spaces in which the heavier exhibits are carefully spaced to allow better photographic views. To give added authenticity in cases of engines which were used on sections with a heavy gradient, the actual gradient has been provided for the display. The museum's pride and joy is the 2–2–2, *Fairy Queen*. Built in 1855 for the East Indian Railway this relic of a wonderful heritage is the oldest surviving locomotive in the world in perfect working order.

Africa

As far as preservation and museums go, Southern Africa contrasts strongly with the north of the continent. Zimbabwee's Railway Museum in Bulawayo and the East African Railway Museum in Nairobi are fine examples of how railway heritage can be preserved, whereas in Ghana, not only is there no preservation, but all semblance of their wonderful railway past has been totally destroyed.

LETADLO BLERIOT ING.KAŠPARA z r.1910
MOTOR DAIMLER 65 KS.

VĚTROŇ
RACEK z r.1936

RAILWAY PRESERVATION GATHERS PACE – BRITAIN AND EUROPE

Britain

When, on 11 August 1968, the curtain was finally drawn on steam on Britain's main line railways it was decreed that no preserved stream locomotive would ever again be allowed to run over British Rail metals. Steam retreated to the confines of a few preserved lines, kept alive by a handful of unpaid, hard-working and dedicated enthusiasts. The 'Return to Steam' Committee was formed and after patient negotiation British Rail climbed down and, in October 1971, to the relief of millions, allowed the restored No. 6000 *King George V*, hauling eight coaches, to make an eight-day tour of the country. As the years went by so the number of steam specials increased until in 1985, an amazing total of 235 steam-hauled excursions operated over Britain's main lines. Today, Britain has upwards of 2,000 locomotives preserved at over 100 centres where steam trains can be enjoyed. Railway preservation is a creative on-going process and as the first generation of diesels began to slip into history, examples of these were also saved and are now put to work on preserved lines, often alongside the very steam locomotives they replaced.

Northern Europe

Northern Europe is richer in presevation than the south. By 1991 Germany had almost 100 preservation societies, such as the Deutscher Eisenbahn-Verein (German Railway Society), which not only maintains its own preserved lines, but also serves as a forum for research and discussion. Others, such as the Deutsche Gesellschaft fur Eisenbahngeschichte (German Railway History Society) have their own static museums with not only locomotives and rolling stock, but also an extensive archive of plans, pictures and literature. In Sweden a similar society is the Jamvags Historiska Riks Forbund which is based in Sundbyberg. Switzerland must be one of the most railway-minded countries in Europe with every Swiss travelling an estimated 1,898km (1,179 miles) a year by train. It is not surprising therefore, that preservation here, over the past 25 years, has grown by leaps and bounds. Not only do the country's two main railway museums, Lucerne and Chaulin, house a wonderful collection of historic locomotives – steam, diesel and electric – but there are also many smaller museums, groups and societies intent on preserving a part of Switzerland's rich railway heritage.

Southern Europe

Although Greece did not open its national museum until 1979, the country is planning further museums in which it is hoped that one of every kind of existing locomotive will be kept, thereby ensuring that no classes are totally lost to posterity. Some of these museums will be built at disused railway stations, such as that proposed at Kalamata. The museum in Athens as well as seven steam locomotives and a collection of railway artefacts and memorabilia, has on show Sultan Abdul Aziz's remarkable smoking car which was built in the 1860s.

Notwithstanding the collection of locomotives in the Milan Leonardo da Vinci Science Museum, Italy also, it would seem, has come late into preservation with its national railway museum in Napels not being opened until 1982. However, there are private organisations which are trying to ensure that Italy's railway past is not forgotten. In Trieste, near the Slovenian border, the organisations Sezione Appassionati Trasporti and Dopolavoro Ferroviario Triestino have combined to establish an extensive collection of locomotives and rolling stock in the historic Campo Marzio station.

The Future?

With national governments accepting that more and more that of the world's cultural and scientific achievements should be kept for future generations, it is hoped that the importance of preservation of our more important historic railways will be officially recognised. This should be in addition to the many enthusiasts who spend their weekends restoring and running preserved lines. The preserved scene has never been healthier and bodes well for the children of the 21st century who will be able to see at first-hand the achievements of their ancestors.

Left: The preservation movement in Britain has been highly active for many years and now steam veterans from Europe can be found running alongside the Castle's, Merchant Navies and Black 5s of British Rail days.

Below: Locomotive 30057 having its side tanks fitted in preparation for its first steaming. The locomotive was repatriated from the USA and after its complete overhaul can be seen running on the Swanage Railway in the south of England.

THE RAILWAY PRESERVATION MOVEMENT IN AMERICA & AUSTRALIA

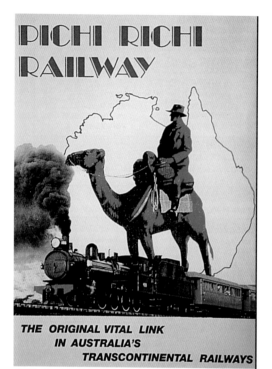

PICHI RICHI RAILWAY

THE ORIGINAL VITAL LINK IN AUSTRALIA'S TRANSCONTINENTAL RAILWAYS

Above: A Poster for the Pich Richi Preservation Railway Society in Australia. Opened in 1879 the line was closed in 1957. It was re-opened as a preservation line in 1973.

Right: Josephine, built by the Vulcan Foundry, Newton-le-Willows, is here housed in Otago Early Settlers' Museum

on New Zealand's South Island.

Below: The Illinois Railway Museum has more than 300 pieces of railway equipment. A pair of former Chicago, North Shore & Milwaukee heavyweight interurban cars pause at the East Union, Illinois depot.

USA

The loss of privately operated intercity passenger services in the United States occurred when Amtrak was formed in 1971 to relieve the railroads of mounting passenger deficits. The great array of colourful passenger trains that once connected the nation was gone, replaced by a skeletal system of homogeneous passenger trains. The nostalgia for the old fashion train ride, combined with the retrenchment of the railroad network, fuelled an interest in railway preservation and spawned dozens of new museums and tourist railroads. Railways that use vintage railroad equipment such as the Valley Railroad in Essex, Connecticut, the Grand Canyon Railway in Arizona, and the Durango & Silverton Narrow Gauge Railroad in Colorado are focused more on the nostalgic train ride, than on the specific preservation of the equipment. Other museums, such as the North Carolina Transportation Museum in Spencer, have focused on the preservation of regional equipment and historic railroad structures. Spencer Shops is a 57-acre complex with 13 buildings including the largest surviving roundhouse in North America, and is home to some 60 pieces of vintage railroad equipment.

Many smaller museums have come about, often with the aim of regional preservation. The Railroad Museum of New England, located near Waterbury, Connecticut has collected diesel electric and electric locomotives along with rolling stock from several New England railroads. Among the more interesting pieces on its roster are an Alco FA cab diesel, General Electric U25b diesel and an E33 electric from the New Haven Railroad.

Today, there are several hundred railway preservation sites and rides in the United States.

Although loosely organised, the American railway preservation movement has secured thousands of pieces of historical railway equipment. Some are beautifully displayed in operating condition, while, sadly, others are in dire need of attention.

Australia

One of the foremost Australian preservation societies is the Puffing Billy Preservation Society which was formed in Easter 1955. The members' aim was to ensure the retention of fan trips, between Upper Ferntree Gully and Belgrave, which had been started by a Melbourne newspaper in December 1954. These trips lasted until February 1958 when, with the expansion of the Melbourne Metropolitan area, the government decided to widen the gauge to Belgrave and electrify the line. Undaunted, the volunteers of the PBPS, again went into battle in an attempt to restore and re-open the balance of the abandoned line. A new station and locomotive depot were built at Belgrave and the line restored to Menzies Creek, where the society established a museum. This work included a two-chain radius deviation around the landslide that had originally caused the line's closure.

Since the recommencement of services in July 1962, the society has grown massively and work is in progress from both ends to complete the line Gembrook. Some of the locomotives preserved by the society include a 2–6–2T, an 1898 American Baldwin, a Taiwanese Shay, an ex-timber line Climax, a Victorian Railways Garratt and a South African Garratt.

With enthusiasts finding it comparatively easy to obtain suitable narrow gauge locomotives and rolling stock from South Africa and Queensland, the Zig Zag Railway was relaid on the well-known but abandoned zigzag route to the west of the Blue Mountains, and now trains are run daily.

As Western Australia ended up with a modern steam locomotive fleet they were hesitant to cut them all up, so these locomotives became available to the enthusiasts. The Australian Railway Historical Society operates a large static museum at Bassendean and runs periodic rail tours. Regular rail tours are also run by the Hotham Valley Railway who have seven steam engines and passenger cars imported from South Africa to augment those obtained locally.

It is not only passenger railways in Australia that are being preserved. The Richmond Main Railway runs ex-coal field locomotives at monthly intervals on an abandoned colliery track.

EAST UNION

SPECIAL RUNS AND LIVING MUSEUMS

MANY VISITORS TO PRESERVED lines have no idea of the years of struggle through which such schemes have gone. The taking over of a derelict system, or in some cases one that had been totally abandoned has, in many cases, often resulted in rebuilding the railway sleeper by sleeper. Railway preservation is achieved only by dedication and hard work, not all neighbours are sympathetic to the cause and planning permission is not always automatic. There are often a considerable number of years between the first stage and the latter and it is only when the line has been restored and all the conditions met, that permission will be given for public runs.

Britain

In Britain, some former stations, such as the Buckinghamshire Railway Centre at Quainton Road near Aylesbury, and former locomotive depots including Didcot in Oxfordshire and Tyseley, Birmingham, have been converted into living museums. These give the visitor an insight into the life of a bygone age, an age in which the railway was the centre of the community which they served. To keep a balance between preservation and the tourism business in which the heritage railways operate, additional buildings and facilities have been sympathetically built where necessary, to enable the ambiance to be retained.

Europe

One of the most interesting live steam museums in Poland is that in Wolsztyn. A feature of the museum, which houses 30 steam locomotives, is the operation of some of these engines on the main line. At nearby Opalenica there is a narrow gauge museum with five locomotives as well as passenger and freight wagons.

The Netherlands also has a number of preserved lines. One of which, just south of Katwijk, is a 3-mile (4.5km) stretch of 700mm gauge line which follows the beautiful North Sea coast. Between June and September visitors can enjoy the wildlife by taking rides in trains which travel through this famous water nature reserve.

At Pforzheim, Germany, between June and October, on a 1,320-yard (1.3km) long reconstructed track, tourists are able to re-live the 1880s by riding in 'Pferdebahnwagon Nr. 21'. This is one of the very few horse-drawn railways operated anywhere in Europe.

USA

Every year, dozens of excursions and fan trips operate in the United States. All sorts of equipment are used and many different lines are featured. Some trips use utilitarian commuter train equipment and common Electro-Motive F40 class diesels, while others use luxurious privately owned classic passenger cars. Occasionally, historic diesels and steam locomotives are used. Charter trips, such as the 'Reno Fun Train' that operates from Oakland, California to Reno, Nevada, are run seasonally with Amtrak equipment over established routes. The 'Fun Train', designed to accommodate holiday travellers heading to the ski area in the Sierra Nevada mountains and to the gambling casinos in Nevada, usually operates once a week in the winter. In Colorado, the 'Rio Grande Ski Train' operates from Denver to Winter Park through the famous Moffat Tunnel using vintage streamlined passenger cars for the benefit of skiers heading to the Front Range.

Many short lines and larger regional railroads provide periodic railroad excursions over their lines for enthusiasts. The Wisconsin Central often uses its business cars in conjunction with privately owned equipment to run passenger excursions. In May 1997, to promote the idea of regular passenger services, the New England Central (which runs the former Central Vermont main line between St Albans, Vermont and New London, Connecticut), operated a series of passenger trips on the southern end of its route.

Regional railroad groups, such as the Amherst Railway Society in Amherst, Massachusetts, sponsor several day-long railroad trips every year, usually on area railroad lines. Privately owned luxury passenger cars, such as the Caritas owned by High Iron Travel in Minneapolis, Minnesota, are available for charters. These cars often run on the back of regularly scheduled Amtrak intercity trains, but also run rare 'mileage' fan trips over selected freight lines.

Above: Pakistan is one of many countries where steam preservation took a back seat many years ago in favour of dieselisation with the exception of the odd special train like this 2–6–2 Prairie with it's flat truck seen running in 1989.

Left: A locomotive No. 6209 *Princess Elizabeth* hauling The Midland Jubilee Rail Tour.

13 *the* **Revolution** *in* **LIGHT RAIL**

THE EVOLUTION OF ELECTRIC TRAMS AROUND THE WORLD

AS WE HAVE ALREADY SEEN, the origin of the tramway can be traced back to the plateways used in mines and quarries to ease the passage of horse-drawn wagons. The first street tramway in a city however, was the New York & Harlem line of 1832. This coined the American term, 'street railway', an expression that is still in use today. Remarkably, the world's second horse tramway, built in 1835 in New Orleans, is still in use today, albeit now operated with electric cars, after over 150 years of continuous service. In 1853, as a result of American promoters, the tramway arrived in Europe, with the opening of the Paris system. Seven years later, in 1860, the first English system was operating in Birkenhead. The following year the first section of London's network was opened. Copenhagen followed in 1863.

Mechanical Traction

The 1870s were a boom time for the construction of horse tramways, but the limitations of animal power were obvious, and promoters soon turned to investigating mechanical traction. Although steam trams were developed and put into operation on many suburban and rural light railways, they were not suitable for urban use. Compressed air, gas and petrol engines were tried; cable tramways enjoyed considerable success for a time (and still survive in San Francisco). However, most of these technically suspect or expensive options faded quickly once electric traction became a possibility.

Electric Traction

The first electric vehicles were battery powered. Then, in 1879, Werner von Siemens demonstrated his new practicable dynamo in Berlin. This provided the way ahead for electric traction which was generated by power at a fixed point from where it was supplied to a line by a conducting rail or overhead wire. The first electric tramway to provide a public service was that opened by Siemens & Halske in Berlin in 1881. This used a 180 volt current that was fed through the running rails. The first lines in the United Kingdom were the Portrush & Bushmills (later Giant's Causeway) Tramway in Ireland, and Volk's Railway at Brighton in 1883. The latter still runs today.

Overhead Wires and Underground Conduits

For safety reasons electrified running rails were unsuitable for a street environment, and overhead wires were first used on the Bessbrook & Newry line in Ireland in 1885. Slotted tube overhead was tried in Paris in 1881. Other European cities included Frankfurt which opened in 1884, and which now has the longest period of continuous electric street tramway operation anywhere in the world, also used this system initially but conventional overhead wire has been used since 1906.

Since poles and overhead wires were not required, underground conduits were sometimes preferred as an alternative to overhead current collection for aesthetic reasons. This system survived in London until the end of tramway operations in 1952, and in Washington DC until 1962. Britain's oldest street tramway, at Blackpool, has operated on an overhead system since 1899 but used conduits when opened in 1885.

The Pantograph

The overhead wire with trolley pole collection was soon shown to be the most practicable solution, and the first city tramway network was that installed by the American, Sprague, in Richmond, Virginia, in 1887. By 1900, almost all US horse tramways had been converted to electric traction, with European cities not far behind. Siemens developed the bow collector as an alternative to the trolley pole and this in turn led to the pantograph which is most common today. Before the end of the 19th century electric tramways had appeared all around the world, including Kyoto, Japan; Bangkok, Thailand and Melbourne, Australia. Tramways in Britain, or those with British heritage stock, usually used double-deck trams to maximise capacity. In mainland Europe, a single-deck tram towing a trailer was more common, while American systems soon progressed to larger trams mounted on two bogies.

Above: A scene from the late 1940s showing one of Leicester's fleet of trams, abandoned in 1949, passing the city's 19th century Clock Tower.

THE DECLINE OF THE TRAM

FOR ABOUT THE FIRST 25 years of the 20th century there was a golden age of tramways. Almost every city of consequence around the world operated a system, mostly under municipal control. The tramway, as well as providing cheap and reliable transport for the masses, also facilitated economic development and the growth of suburbs. Technical innovation in electrical and mechanical engineering permitted larger and more powerful cars, and high-speed interurban lines sprang up, particularly in North America where over 15,000 miles (24,000km) of line criss-crossed the continent.

By the 1920s, however, some tramway managers were worried men. There had been a rapid increase in the cost of labour and materials and politicians were usually reluctant to face fare increases to match. The initial investment was wearing out, but on the systems the profits of the good years had been hived off, with insufficient thought given to retaining funds for the renewal of equipment. Mass production of motor cars was starting and reliable motor buses were becoming available. All this meant that real competition was looming at a time when it was cheaper to introduce bus feeders than extend the existing tramways.

Motor Bus Competition

The Depression, which started in America in 1929, soon affected European economies and caused a rapid collapse of not only many small town tramways, but also most interurban networks. These were systems that operated at marginal profitability and were thus prone to the effects of competition. The motor bus took over and from the early 1930s the trolley bus provided a way of contemplating tramway abandonment without dispensing with the electrical supply infrastructure. In the United States, where municipal ownership was less common, there is considerable evidence of a concerted effort by the bus and oil companies to take over ailing tramways and replace them with bus routes to boost the profits of both groups. Ironically, within little more than a decade, those profits had disappeared under the tidal wave of mass private motoring and many municipalities had to step in to ensure the retention of some vestige of public transport.

Above: A derelict tram lies abandoned at Harbin depot, China. After being gradually cut back over recent years, the final short stretch of line succumbed to buses in 1987.

The PCC Car

The tramway managers did not give in without a fight. In North America the Presidents' Congress Committee of Streetcar Companies commissioned research and production of a new design of tram that would offer motor car levels of comfort and performance. The result was the PCC car, which staved off the closure of many systems, and saved others, to form the basis of a tramway revival of the modern age. Indeed, some still operate today, and

have become an icon for those interested in heritage tramways as a contribution to urban regeneration. The PCC arrived in Europe during the late 1940s. One line that was modified was the United Kingdom's pioneer Blackpool Tramway. This was modernised with large numbers of trams built to the PCC principles, and so ensured the survival of that system to the present day.

World War II hastened the decline of tramways in the United Kingdom and France, but provided the opportunity for reconstruction and reinvestment in the Benelux countries, Germany and Eastern Europe. In Britain the nationalisation of the municipal electrical supply was another reason for the attractions of cheap motor buses to sound the death knell for the tramways. Some city systems, such as Glasgow and Liverpool, enjoyed a post-war renaissance, with fleets of new trams and reserved-track extensions, but never enough to ensure they became a dominant part of the network. The last British city system to close was at Glasgow in 1962.

Below: A scrapyard scene at St Denys, Southampton, England, in June 1949. The low built open topped cars with their back-to-back 'knifeboard' seats on top were designed to fit under the town's medieval Bargate Arch.

Above and Right:
These busy street
scenes show how
much pollution can
be caused by exhaust
fumes. Public
transport can go a
long way to making
the world's cities
cleaner and healthier.

THE 1960s WERE BAD YEARS for public transport in many parts of the world. The growing belief by industry and planners was that the motor car would become the ordinary form of transport for most people, with buses for those who could not afford cars. They also contended that cities could be adapted to cope with the increased traffic that would result. By 1962, the only system left in Britain was that in Blackpool, which, with its unique traffic patterns, remained faithful to the tram that had its reserved track on the sea front. A handful of tramway systems survived in North American cities, though many believed that bus replacement was just a matter of time. Elsewhere around the world, tramway modernisation had come to a stop as the economics of mass production disappeared from the tramway supply market.

Germany

Only on mainland Europe did investment in tramways continue, particularly in Northern and Eastern Europe. Although countries, such as Spain, France and Italy, all followed the abandonment trend, West Germany became the centre of world tramway development with the German manufacturer Duewag achieving prominence in the field of tramcar design. In particular, Germany played a leading role in the progress of articulated trams. These were eventually operated by one person, with most fares collected off the car by season ticket sales or ticket machines at stops. Frequent ticket inspections ensured the viability of the honour fare system.

Only by means of constant improvement in the ratio of passengers to staff did the tram continue to demonstrate superior economics to the bus and, despite an increase in car ownership, the modernised fleets and infrastructure encouraged patronage. In many city centres in Austria, Belgium and Germany the tram was kept free of the worst effects of traffic congestion by the construction of shallow subway systems under busy crossroads or crowded streets.

Eastern Europe

The Benelux countries and Eastern Europe became the home of the Europeanised PCC car which attracted traffic by its high performance and frequent service. As the communist regimes of Eastern Europe had little private motoring, the development of high-capacity public transport was of prime importance. Another factor was that as full metro systems (underground railways) were unaffordable outside the major conurbations, the tramway would become the dominant mode for city transport. Due to centralised planning the Soviet Union became the world's largest tramway operator, with Leningrad (St Petersburg) having the most extensive tramway network in the world. In the 1960s, the most prolific

tramcar manufacturer anywhere was the Czecho-slovakian firm CKD Tatra of Prague. As Comecon agreements made them the supplier for most of Eastern Europe and the Soviet Union, the company's production reached 1,000 cars a year.

The Decline of the City Centre

By the end of the 1960s the more far-sighted of the planners in the West had begun to realise the disadvantages of wholesale dependence on motor cars and the resulting reduction of public transport. In some major cities peak time traffic congestion was reaching chaotic proportions. In an attempt to cope with the ever-increasing demands of private motoring, attempts to create new super highways in urban areas were seeing whole swathes of cities demolished or divided – a phenomenon that brought both economic and social decline.

This was particularly the case in North America. Here, many cities saw a rapid decline in their city centres as new suburban malls, focused almost entirely on travel by car, sprang up to serve populations that had migrated from high to low density housing areas in the suburbs. Concerns about environmental pollution started to surface. Planners and politicians began to look at flourishing cities in Continental Europe for a solution to their problems and realised the importance of effective public transport, such as that provided by reserved-track tramways.

Below: A tram makes its way through snow-swept Volgograd. The Soviet Union laid great store on public transport; notice the road is completely devoid of private cars.

THE REVIVAL OF THE STREETCAR or tram in North America, usually in the guise of light rail, has been just as remarkable as it has been in Europe. The Americans' love affair with the automobile may not be over, but they have at least realised that it is not possible to rebuild major cities to accommodate unrestrained traffic growth, either in social or environmental terms. Pressures for better public transport as an alternative to the private car are particularly strong in California, where the West Coast ethos is particularly suitable for political initiatives to this end.

Light Rail Vehicles

In the 1970s American urban planners started to look to Europe for ideas on how to save their cities from sprawl and economic decline. With transportation companies now in public ownership, the introduction of better public transport could be achieved using a mix of city, state and national funding. At the same time, with the end of the Vietnam War, defence contractors were looking for alternative markets and saw transportation as a growth area. This led to a decision by the surviving tramway cities of Boston and San Francisco to place orders for new articulated light rail vehicles (LRVs) with Boeing-Vertol. These used a design that was intended to become the standard US LRV in the same way that the PCC had achieved standardisation 40 years earlier. Unfortunately, the resulting product was a technical disaster, as Boeing tried to 'reinvent the wheel' rather than learning from experience elsewhere.

The Canadian city of Edmonton led the way with an alternative approach of adapting European technology to American conditions. They built a new light rail line, partly on under-used railway alignment and partly in city subways, and operated it, from 1978, with imported trams from Siemens-Duewag in Germany. This approach was an immediate success, and was soon copied by both San Diego and Calgary. In these cases, rather than dig expensive subways, pedestrian and transit precincts were created in the city centres, since guided pollution-free vehicles such as trams can operate quite successfully in pedestrian areas.

New Lines, New Rolling Stock

The success of these systems in attracting back to public transit motorists who would not dream of using a bus, led to a boom in the development and construction of light rail systems which is still going on today. Baltimore, Buffalo, Dallas, Denver, Los Angeles, Portland, Sacramento and St Louis are all cities that have built new light rail lines, many of which are still expanding. New systems are under construction in Jersey City and Salt Lake City, with progress in other cities such as New York and Seattle. The systems at Cleveland, Pittsburgh and Philadelphia, which survived from the earlier street car era have all acquired new rolling stock and are expanding again.

The example of Los Angeles is particularly significant, since this was a city that threw away its trams and interurbans in the 1960s, determined that it could live with the automobile. The pall of pollution that hangs over the urban sprawl proves differently and two new light rail lines have been opened, with a third under construction.

South of the border, new light rail lines have been built in Guadalajara, Monterey and Mexico DF. In South America tramways had virtually disappeared by the end of the 1960s, but the first new light rail lines have now appeared in Buenos Aires and Rio de Janeiro.

Left: Los Angeles' Flower Street is one of the many stops on this, California's largest light rail network.

Below: Portland, Oregon's new light rail system is still expanding. Built to ease traffic congestion, its ease of operation appeals to many motorists who would not dream of taking a bus.

METROS IN EUROPE

Gothenburg Leads the Way

Light rail was first created in mainland Europe as street tramways were upgraded with new rolling stock and track segregated from public roadways. The concept owes much to the planning which took place in Gothenburg, Sweden where, over a period of 15 years, an ordinary city street tramway was extended through new and established suburbs on high-speed reserved track. At the same time, every encouragement to use public transport was given. All the rolling stock was replaced with a fleet of high-performance trams, and by introducing effective traffic restrictions, which gave priority to trams in the central area. This was achieved without the expense of boring any tunnels, thereby keeping public transport on the surface as a visible and accessible system.

Since 1980, many cities have chosen to follow the same path. Graz and Linz in Austria, Amsterdam in the Netherlands, Basle and Zurich in Switzerland and Ghent in Belgium are good examples. Elsewhere in Belgium, Germany and Austria, it was thought that the best way of improving the average speed of public transport in city streets was to provide a segregated path in subways. Cities such as Antwerp, Brussels, Cologne, Hanover, Stuttgart and Vienna provide examples of this approach. Recently the cost of underground construction has become prohibitive and there has been a swing back to imposing restrictions on motor traffic as a way of achieving public transport priority on the surface.

The upgraded systems have created new terminology to differentiate them from ordinary tramways – Supertram, Light Rail, Metro, *Sneltram* (express tram) and *Stadtbahn* (town rail) are some of the names used. Some German upgraded subway tramways are marketed in the same was as underground metros by using the term *U-Bahn* (underground railway). Another aspect of the subway's popularity in the 1970s and 1980s was that it permitted level boarding of high-floor cars in the city suburbs. On surface lines in the suburbs, there was often space available to install platforms level with the vehicle floor making them accessible for passengers in wheelchairs, or those with prams and buggies. Elsewhere the cars use their fold-down steps.

Light Rail in Britain

Legislation in the 1960s provided the groundwork for progress towards a new era in public transport. Local authorities were charged with developing plans for integrated transport systems. In the major conurbations, Passenger Transport Executives (PTEs) were created to take over responsibility for operation and development of public transport in their area.

In the north west of England, the Tyne & Wear PTE published its public transport plan in 1973. This set out proposals for the creation of a light rail transit system to take over the alignment of 26 miles (42km) of run-down local railway lines and link them up with 8½ miles (13.5km) of new infrastructure. This created a network of electrified suburban lines that formed the core of an integrated passenger transport system. The initial route was opened in stages from 1980 to 1984. This, Britain's first modern light rail system, has been successful in assisting the regeneration of Tyneside and carries over 40 million passengers a year.

In London, a key issue in the proposed regeneration of the docklands area east of the city was public transport. Light rail was selected as an appropriate and affordable option in 1982. The initial seven-mile (12km) long system has since been extended to 13 miles (22km) and is now being further extended to south of the Thames. Such is the network's popularity that over 22 million passengers a year are carried.

Many of Britain's major cities are planning to use a range of systems, from segregated and automated operation on former rail alignments, to conventional street tramways.

Left: A Network South East train leaves London over Blackfriars Bridge. Metro systems often link with the major railway stations easing road congestion within large cities.

Low-Floor Trams

In the 1990s, new technology was developed which provides low-floor trams with step-free entrances only 350mm above rail level. Surface systems achieved exactly the same effect just by building up kerbs slightly, to a matching height. This is now the favoured solution for making trams fully accessible, and over 2,000 low-floor cars have been delivered or ordered for European systems. In Britain, all new systems are required to offer step-free access to trams, resulting in new rolling stock which will be supplied by Belgium, German and Italian manufacturers.

In countries such as France, Italy and Spain which, like Great Britain had abandoned their tramway heritage, there has also been a swing back to trams. France has led the way with new systems in Nantes, Grenoble, Paris and Rouen. All these systems are fully accessible in their entirety thanks to their low–floor tram fleets. Other systems are planned for Bordeaux, Montpelier, Orleans and Toulon. The Spanish city of Valencia has similarly built a new tramway and others are developing plans. In Italy, Genoa has a new segregated light rail line and many cities are planning tramway systems with the support of companies.

AUSTRALIA, ASIA AND AFRICA

Above: **The Tin Shui Wai Terminus in Hong Kong. This former Crown Colony is rapidly updating its old light rail system and building new metro lines. Here one of the region's trams passes some of the tall apartment blocks which are so common here.**

Right: **Light rail is not common in Africa. Tunis is one of only two countries in the continent where it can be found. Here we see one of their German-built articulated cars passing through the suburbs.**

Australia and New Zealand

The antipodean tram was largely modelled on its British counterpart, though double-deckers were less common. There was a rapid decline in the 1950s and 1960s as small-town systems closed for economic reasons, while at the same time cities such as Adelaide, Brisbane and Sydney gave up trams for industro-political reasons. However, the largest system, 137 miles (220km) long, in the southern hemisphere, at Melbourne, survived intact, thanks to good management and political support. The first new trams for 20 years arrived in 1975. Since then a total of 362 new cars have transformed the system from a very traditional and conservative operation to one that is much more customer orientated and which is being prepared for privatisation. Several new extensions have been built and two local rail lines converted to light rail operation and linked by street operation with the city centre.

The return of trams to Melbourne's great rival, Sydney, took place in 1997 with the opening of a short line built and operated by the private sector. This will form the basis of an expanded network, including operation in city streets, by the time the Olympic Games are held in the city in the year 2000. Elsewhere, Brisbane is considering the introduction of trams and the surviving route to Adelaide is due to be modernised. This line was due for extension in the 1980s, but a change of political power saw the introduction of the German O-Bahn guided bus-way system.

In New Zealand, trams had disappeared from the city streets by the 1960s. However, 1995 saw their return to Christchurch in the form of a heritage loop through the city centre using museum cars to provide a tourist–orientated service. Light rail is also on the agenda in Auckland and Wellington.

Asia

As Japan has suffered even more from the mass usage of private cars than the USA and Western Europe, conditions have not been conducive to the survival of the street tramway. However, many tramways have been steadily upgraded over the years to run on segregated alignments. These form the basis of a substantial network of electric light railways that are an important part of the well-patronised public transport network. Ironically,

some small town street tramway operations have survived and are slowly being modernised. The first low-floor tram, based on a German design, was introduced in 1997. Elsewhere in Asia, rail-based urban public transport is less common. India's only surviving tramway, in Calcutta, is a large network, but years of under-investment have left services in a parlous state. By contrast the capital of the Philippines, Manila, opened a new segregated light rail line across the city in 1984. The success of this has encouraged the construction of two more lines using private capital. China had little tramway operation, and just three Manchurian towns operate trams today. In 1997 the People's Republic acquired the British colony of Hong Kong, where British-style double-deck trams have run since 1904, and continue to compete successfully with intensive bus operation on the streets of Hong Kong Island. A complete contrast is the 20-mile (32km) long light rail system, built since 1988, in the suburban township of Tuen Mun. This is one of the most heavily patronised rail systems in the world and carries over 112 million passengers a year. The North Korean capital of Pyongyang has built a new tramway system and in Malaysia a new light metro system opened in 1996.

Africa

In Africa, light rail is limited to Tunisia and Egypt. Tunis has created a 20-mile (32km) long system since 1985 with German-built articulated cars operating on four surface lines that carry 90 million passengers a year. Alexandria has a street tramway and a suburban light rail line while Cairo, Heliopolis and Helwan, operate modernised light rail lines.

The Flexibility of Light Rail

Light rail systems are not a rigidly defined concept, but a flexible mode that fits between the bus and the heavy metro, or conventional railway, and can be operated like any of them. In comparison with a system of buses on city streets, it is more expensive to construct, but may be cheaper to operate for a given capacity. It also has lower whole-life costs, a higher commercial speed, produces less pollution and can be more successful in attracting motorists to public transport. In comparison with a metro or urban railway, light rail will be cheaper to build and operate, but runs at a lower speed. However, it will maintain a visible presence of public transport, offer better penetration of urban areas, enjoy better security and generate less noise. Light rail can cater economically and effectively for passenger flows between 2,000 and 20,000 passengers an hour and this will usually be found in cities with populations between 200,000 and one million.

Light rail usually involves steel wheeled vehicles running on steel rails and collecting electrical power from an overhead wire. Diesel light rail is a concept that has been tried to a limited extent and may have a role in the future for low-cost starter lines. The steel rails can be grooved, so that they may lay flush with a street surface, or ballasted like normal railway track. This makes light rail the only system that can operate on both city streets and jointly with conventional rail services. It also offers the possibility that regional rail services can be extended through to the city centre by way of transfer points from rail to street track. This idea, which has been introduced with enormous success in Karlsruhe, Germany, using dual voltage light rail vehicles, is now being built elsewhere.

Light rail also demonstrates its flexibility by its ability to operate in a wide range of built-up environments. It can act as a tramway in the street, though if its advantages over the bus are to be maximised, unsegregated street track should be kept to a minimum, such as at narrow points without room for a tram reservation.

Within public streets the track can be segregated by white lines, low kerbs and side or central reservations. Tracks can be laid in tarmac, mass concrete, ballast or grass, according to operational and environmental needs. Light rail can be built on former railway formations, or indeed use track shared with railways, whether little used freight lines or those with a passenger service. Technical progress means that appropriate safety arrangements can be put into force for mixed services despite the differing buffing loads of light rail and heavy rail rolling stock.

Heritage Tramways

Although light rail is a modern mass transit system for cities, trams are being used increasingly to put the fun back into inner city life. A score of American cities have discovered just how a heritage tramway can be an economical boost to the central area, and the trend has spread to Europe. These heritage tramways, run with restored or replica cars, can share tracks with light rail services and are often entirely separate from preservation activities by museum groups, although the two can interrelate quite successfully. Many established tramway systems run tourist-orientated services, such as the very successful Melbourne City Circle line. Other systems are stand-alone, such as the heritage line opened in 1995 for Birkenhead in England, which uses replica double-deckers built in Hong Kong. Trams and light rail covering the range of public transport provision and international experience of 150 systems worldwide confirm that this is the most successful intermediate mode of public transport, with over 100 years of development behind it, yet incorporating the latest technology for the future.

Above: In common with most former communist countries, Hungary concentrated more on providing public transport than on the maintenance of roads. Budapest has a fine light rail network, which makes getting about in that city incredibly easy.

Left: The Milan tram network is extremely popular with all generations.

14 the **Railway's** **role** in the **MODERN** **world**

PBKAL

In Europe one of the most exciting railway ventures, as the Millennium draws near, is that which is being undertaken by the Netherlands, Belgium, France, Germany and Britain. Centred in Belgium, the ten year plan, which commenced in 1996, allows for high speed rail projects that will unit Paris, Brussels, Cologne (Köln), Amsterdam and London. This PBKAL project is advancing rapidly and it is hoped that all the links will be in full operation by 2005, some, such as Brussels to Antwerp and Brussels to Liège by 2002. In Antwerp a major tunnelling project is planned to connect the north and south rail termini which is expected to be complete by 2003.

A Railway Culture

Although many of the new railway developments have been in Western Europe, the promotion of what can be loosely termed a 'railway culture' has not been confined to the richer countries in the northern hemisphere. In the Third World many railways have been constructed as a consequence of the need to exploit mineral or natural resources, such as in Brazil where new routes into the rain forests are being constructed. The building of such new infrastructure has, however, to be balanced by the environmental consequences of the opening up of the interior. In Africa, railway development has been patchy, and though newly independent nations have invested in railways, the situation has not been helped by political instability, civil war and constant lack of finance.

China

In China, the construction of new railways has been a phenomenon unmatched anywhere else in the world. Since 1949, the country's network has grown by more than 30,000 miles (48,270km). Indeed, plans are now in hand for a new underground railway in the southern city of Shenzhen. The 9½-mile (15km) system will run beneath the busy routes of Renmin Road and Shennan Road to the suburban town of Futian, linking Lowu and Lok Ma Chau. This futuristic system will enable passengers from Hong Kong to reach the heart of the city in about 20 minutes.

In Hong Kong, construction is expected to start in late 1998 on the region's new West Rail Phase 1 Project. When completed, this exciting 21st century, double-tracked electrified system will go the 21 miles (34km) from Yen Chow Street in Kowloon to Tuen Mun. A feature of the line is that 8½ miles (13.7km) will be underground and a further 5½ miles (8.8km) will be elevated. In this way the railway will not interfere with the flow of heavy road traffic, to which the former Crown Colony is prone. The line is envisaged to have nine stations, including two which will have interchanges with the Kowloon to Peking main line.

Pollution

As the resurgence of railways has continued in the world community, in the West there has been a gradual change in attitudes towards road transport. Recent estimates have suggested that by the year 2025 there will be ten million more cars on the road in Britain and there is a growing recognition that an integrated transport policy is a very high priority. What is emerging is that rather than dominating transport policy as they once did, railways should become a key partner in an integrated approach to the creation of a transport system that serves the needs of the population.

Concern over levels of traffic congestion and pollution has led to railways being challenged to offer a service that is clean, convenient, affordable and efficient. It is only if they can provide this that they will be able to persuade drivers to leave their cars at home and use public transport. The growth and importance of light rail and metro tram systems in the world's largest cities have shown that although railways can make a difference to the quality of life for urban population, a great deal of work still remains to be done.

Below: One of the trains on the new 34km long railway that connects Hong Kong's new Chek Lap Kok airport, on Lantau Island, with downtown Kowloon. It is the first purpose-built railway to serve an airport with in-town-check-in facilities at its major stations.

FREIGHT

Above: A Class 60 of Railfreight origin hauls a heavy aggregate train through the English countryside.

FROM THE 1960s THE TRADITIONAL method of sending goods by train in individual wagons declined dramatically. Outdated methods of handling freight, dating back to the 19th century, in which railways concentrated on the running of bulk trains of one particular load, be it coal or consumer goods, allowed road competition to steal away business. The carrying of bulk loads has to be one of the strongest arguments for railway development, for every load transported by rail reduces the number of lorries on the world's congested road networks. The movement of coal, stone and other loads has become largely the province of rail and improvements in technology have allowed longer and heavier trains to be moved. Today, as we have seen, coal is moved from pit to power station in 'merry-go-round' trains which load and unload on the move. Large amounts of limestone are also moved by rail as are other bulk loads such as oil, petroleum, iron ore and steel.

One-Mile Long Trains

In the United States and other parts of the world, the bulk loads carried by rail dwarf anything seen on European railways. The Burlington Northern Railroad introduced a train that consisted of over a hundred 100-ton wagons, with a load of over 11,000 tons. In South Africa, trains of up to 19,840 tons are hauled the 537 miles (864km) from the iron ore mines at Sishen in Cape Province, to the coast at Saldanha. A unique feature of these trains is that a motorcycle is 'garaged' on each of the five locomotives. This is used to make regular inspections of the train which can be over 1½ mile (2.4km) in length.

'Piggyback' Trains

In the search for new ways of increasing freight business railway companies have investigated more unorthodox methods. 'Piggyback' trains, also known as TOFC ('Trailers On Flat Cars'), which originated in the United States, allow lorry trailer units to be carried on flat wagons. In 1967 the Atchison, Topeka & Santa Fe Railroad introduced the 'Super C' service, which claimed to be the world's fastest freight train. In the 1970s it was calculated that US and Canadian railroads were handling nearly two million 'piggyback' loads per year. Difficulties with loading gauges precluded the use of such innovations in Britain until very recently, but in 1996 proposals were put forward for 'piggyback' trains to be in operation by 1999.

Containerisation

Another innovation that has transformed railway freight is the introduction of containerisation. The widespread use of containers for the movement of goods all over the world and their adaptability for transport by ship, rail or lorry has been a revolution. In the United States enormous trains of containers move from coast to coast, since it is cheaper to move them by rail than to ship them through the Panama Canal. The staggering scale of this business may be judged by the fact that the train is over a mile long, and is hauled by six locomotives. Container traffic in Britain was originally given the brand name 'Freightliner' by British Rail, and today is still a key part of the railway business, especially with the opening of the Channel Tunnel.

Integrated Transport Links

The idea of integrated transport links is also extremely relevant in the freight business today with more and more regional 'intermodal' freight depots being built or planned. One such is the new DIRFT depot in the East Midlands, which links the international railway system to the road network. In this way both forms of transport can work together more harmoniously for the benefit of all parts of the community.

Left: A diesel electric of the Norfolk Southern railroad hauls a piggyback train at Cumberland Falls, Kentucky.

Below: A heavy freight hauled by a Canadian National diesel electric passing the signals at Marysville, Ontario.

The Train à Grande Vitesse (TGV)

TGV trains travel so fast that special lines had to be laid with greater than normal spacing between the tracks to reduce the buffeting which ensues when the trains pass each other. Another feature of the line is that they stick close to the land contours thereby, in many cases, avoiding the need for tunnels. The tracks are also built with a special cant that allows curves to be negotiated safely. Travel on the TGV, between Paris and Berne, is so smooth that not only is the impression of the high speed hard to judge, but there is also little chance to study the local scenery. This journey takes a breathtaking 4 hours 32 minutes. Combining Eurostar and TGV, a traveller can leave London at the civilised hour of 09.53, arrive in Paris at 14.08 (Central European Time), leave at 15.50 and be in Berne by 20.22. In 1990, a TGV achieved a world speed record travelling at 320.19mph (515.3kph).

A feature of the early TGV trains was the elongated nose. More modern ones are less angular. They are able to collect current at 1,500V dc as well as 25,000V ac. The redesign has made them more aerodynamic with weight being saved by making some parts from aluminium. Another feature of the train is the electronic device that continuously monitors the line's profile. When it senses a change, it adjusts the power input to the traction motors to maintain the speed set by the driver. While first class travellers on the TGV can enjoy luxurious semi-compartment seating, second class passengers have not been forgotten. Not only are there two areas of seating bays which families can use, but also a play area, nursery and special accommodation for the disabled.

Eurostar

Although the international group responsible for the design of Eurostar adopted the principles employed in the French TGV, numerous changes were necessary. The main one was that, as it had to operate in various countries, it had to be capable of using the electrical supply from three different systems, including current collection from a third rail in Britain. The exterior design was British, while the interior design was a joint French and Belgian operation.

There were many mechanical and electrical problems to be solved. For example, safety requirements for the Channel Tunnel demanded that passengers could be moved from one end of the whole train to the other. This ruled out employing two units. Eurostar has just two power cars that are situated at each end of the 20-vehicle formation. To make up, to some extent, for the loss of power which two equivalent TGV sets would have had, additional motored bogies are situated under the first and last passenger coach. The bogies had to be reduced in overall dimensions and the high overhead contact line in the Tunnel called for a higher reaching pantograph. Other requirements were for the footsteps to be designed so as to match the differing heights of platforms in three countries automatically, and the problems of various complex signalling arrangements had to be solved. It is, therefore, a credit to the international teams that this was all achieved between conception in 1987 and the start of regular services in November 1994.

The Channel Tunnel, which lies 377ft (137.4m) below mean sea level, is 31.03 miles (49.93km) long and as such is the longest underwater tunnel in the world. Passage through the Tunnel takes about 20 minutes. It is on the fatest section between Calais and Paris that Eurostar is able to run at its maximum authorised speed of

Left: The aerodynamic lines of the high-speed Class 373 electric Eurostar, which has cut the rail journey time between London and Paris to under four hours.

Below: The eye-catching livery of the trans-continental Thalys is shown at Cologne during running trials for the service.

THE JAPANESE SHINKANSEN 'BULLET TRAIN'

THE COMPLETION OF JAPAN'S Shinkansen Railway, Tokaido line in 1960 heralded a new era in rail transportation. For the past 21 years the world record for the highest scheduled speed had been held by Italy, when in July 1939 a three-car articulated set ran the 195.8 miles (315.04km) between Florence and Milan at an average speed of 102mph (164kph). Japan's new railway was designed to operate at 130mph (209kph).

Specially constructed to permit high speeds, Japan's high-speed railway was built with no curve with a radius less than 1½ miles (2km). In an age before 'environmentally friendly' was commonplace, the Japanese, in an effort to both avoid urban congestion and to minimise noise, carried the line on viaducts with high parapet walls some 21ft (6.4 metres) above towns. There are no level crossings on the track, and valleys and estuaries are all crossed on long viaducts. Where mountains blocked the way no less than 66 tunnels, twelve of which over 1½ miles (2km) long, were driven through the solid rock. As with the French TGV, to allow for the aerodynamic effect of two trains passing at speeds of over 250mph (400kph), the distance between the nearest rails of opposing tracks in the tunnels has been increased from the standard 6ft (1.8m) to between 9ft (2.7m) and 9ft 6in (2.89m). At the time of writing, from 06.00 to 21.00, a Hikari (Lightning) train leaves Tokyo for Osaka every 15 minutes and covers the 322 miles (518km) in three hours and 10 minutes. Stopping only twice, at Nagoya and Kyoto, each 16-car train, with an average of 1,000 passengers, travels at an average speed of over 100mph (160kph). Advanced and futuristic as it is, the Hikari has now been superseded by the Nozomi 500 which entered service in March 1997. This unmistakable train makes one round trip between Osaka and Hakata daily and regularly operates at speeds up to 186mph (300kph). The fastest regularly scheduled train in the world, this is a journey that no visitor to Japan should miss.

The Russian Sokol

In Russia, the share-holding company, High-Speed Railways, in co-operation with the Ministry of Railways of the Russian Federation are developing a new high-speed passenger electric train named 'Sokol'. Under consideration since 1987, designed by the Central Construction Bureau of Marine Engineering (RUBIN), the train is being built by Transmash Ltd at their Tikhvin plant. The ecologically clean train is designed to carry over 800 passengers, in both tourist and business class, with speeds of between 155 and 217mph (250 and 350kph). The 1,059ft (322.8m) long train will have 12 cars and is designed for two kinds of traction power – 3kV dc and of 25kV ac. There will be 16 3-phase induction motors each of 675kW with a continuous power of 10,800kW. Passengers will be catered for by a refreshment car, international telephone and special seats for disabled passengers. Although primarily designed for use on the new specialised high-speed main line between St Petersburg and Moscow, it is also designed to be handled, with speeds of up to 125mph (200kph), on more conventional railways. By the year 2010 it is planned to have produced 150 sets of these fascinating trains.

Not only is work continuing on the train but also special termini are being built. In July 1997, work began on constructing the new terminal next to the Moscow station in St Petersburg and, at the other end of the line, Moscow's Riga station is to be redeveloped.

Above: An artist's impression of the High Speed Sokol Train which will run on the proposed Moscow to St Petersburg high-speed railway. The Russian Duma approved the project in June 1997.

Above: The JR500 is the latest of a line of so-called 'Bullet Trains' which operate at speeds of up to 300kph on Japan's Shinkansen, a new high-speed railway.

INTO THE 21ST CENTURY

Above: An artist's impression of the rolling stock for the Midland Metro which will run between Birmingham and Wolverhampton. Currently under construction this is the latest scheme in the English revival of light rail.

MANY RAILWAYS HAVE BEEN operating automatic signalling systems since the early 20th century. Today, with many new rapid transport systems being computer-based, automatic route-setting has been combined with other functions to produce fully automatic systems. However, as advanced as these systems are, most trains still need an operator to ensure that the train is ready to depart and to give the starting signal, as sell as being a deterrent to vandals.

Lille

The world's first totally unmanned train was the VAL (Véhicule Automatique Légère) rapid transit system in Lille, France, which was opened in April 1983, by President Mitterand. It is a fully automatic rapid-transit system part elevated, part on the surface and part underground. The stations on this futuristic system are also unstaffed. For passenger safety the platforms have continuous glass panelling along the edge with automatic sliding doors which open simultaneously with those of the train when it has come to a standstill.

The rubber-tyred two-car trains are driven automatically on concrete runways which are spaced 5ft 3in (1.6m) apart. There are times, however, when the cars have to be manually driven. For these occasions there is a small control panel at each end, which enables staff to manoeuvre the vehicles in areas such as maintenance depots.

Vancouver

Vancouver's fully automated Skytrain was built to provide a link between the city's two Expo 86 sites. Opened in December 1985, it was so named because much of the original 6½-mile (10.4km) long route was over viaducts, including a stretch over a new cable-stayed bridge spanning the Fraser River. Like the Lille system, the trains are nominally unstaffed, however, roving staff are there both to discourage vandalism and to render assistance to the public. The aluminium cars, which weigh 14 tons, can carry 40 seated passengers and up to 68 standing. As a safety precaution, the first train each day, while driven automatically, carries a member of staff, stationed in the front of the car, ready to make an emergency stop should any object have fallen onto the track during the shut-down period.

London, England

Like the French and Canadian systems London's Docklands Light Railway, opened by HM Queen Elizabeth II in 1987, is fully automatic. However, unlike the other two systems the DLR was a purely political venture, intended to attract industry to the former dock areas of London. Also, unlike the French and Canadian systems, each train carries a 'train captain' whose job it is to check tickets and assist the public. The 'captain' also gives the starting signal to the control computer and, in an emergency, drives the train from a set of controls at the front of the vehicle.

The Computer Age

In today's computer age trains are being revolutionised by being fitted with micro processors which enable faults and failures to be detected and prevented. Locomotives are equipped with on-board computers which enable the data to be read direct or transferred to the maintenance depot for action.

A Vision of the End of the 20th Century

In the 1890s Gustav Eifel, he of the eponymous Parisian landmark, looked into the future and, with Wellsian insight, gave his artistic impressions of how he believed the world would be at the end of the 20th century. Most of these do not concern us here. However, one does. That is the electric train which would convey passengers from Paris to Peking. Seeing the direct line to Turkey opening, he believed that a line would, by the year 2000, exist from one side of the world's largest land mass to the other. Although his design is obviously based on late 19th century technology, his design of the electric multiple unit was well ahead of its time. Were it not for political reasons his dream might well have come true – it might yet.

Above: The Dockland's Light Railway in London was one of the first of the new light rail lines in the UK which use highly sophisticated control and guidance systems. It runs through the heart of the old dock's area of the city, now redeveloped into a high tech village with a mix of commercial and dwelling accommodation. Here the line is seen at Bow Church.

GLOSSARY

APT Advanced Passenger Train.

Amtrak The US passenger carrying railway organisation.

Articulated locomotive A locomotive which has two independent sets of frames joined together with independent groups of wheels.

Atlantics Steam locomotives of 4–4–2 wheel arrangement.

Bankers Sometimes called helpers, these are locomotives whose purpose it is to ease heavy trains over mountainous terrain.

Block Signalling A system whereby only one train is allowed in one section of line at any one time.

Bo–Bo A diesel wheel arrangement whereby 'Bo' indicates a four-wheeled driving axle.

Boxpok wheels A fabricated solid wheel as opposed to spoked.

Camelbacks These locomotives were so-called because the cab was mounted in the centre of the boiler above the driving wheels giving the appearance of a camel's hump.

Catenary The cable in an overhead electrification system which supports the conductor wire.

Co–Co A diesel wheel arrangement whereby 'Co' indicates a six-wheeled driving axle.

Crane Tanks Tank engines fitted with a crane above the boiler, mainly used in dockyards for lifting heavy loads.

Decapod A locomotive of 2–10–0 wheel arrangement

DMU Diesel Multiple Unit.

EMU Electrical Multiple Unit.

Feldbahn A type of German locomotive of World War I.

Fell system of braking A system of braking which works from a centre rail that retards the locomotive and train whilst working on heavily graded lines.

Flying Hamburger A German express diesel of the 1930s.

Gauge The distance between one rail and the other.

Haystack Fireboxes Tall fireboxes resembling a haystack.

Hydraulic transmission The control of water or other liquid flow through pipes.

Kriegslok 'War Locomotive'. German locomotives of World War II.

Maglev A vehicle which runs above the tracks by means of magnetic levitation.

Mallet Compound locomotives first designed by Swiss engineer Anatole Mallet in 1873.

'Merry-go-round' trains A train which is loaded as it slowly moves under the loading hoppers.

Mikado A locomotive of 2–8–2 wheel arrangement.

Mixed Traffic A locomotive which is designed to work both fast passenger or heavy goods trains.

Outshopped Leaving the works.

Pacific Steam locomotives of 4–6–2 wheel arrangement

Pendolinos™ An Italian high-speed train made by Fiat.

Piggyback Operation The conveyance by rail of road vehicles on flat wagons.

Plinth A method of displaying a locomotive at a static location.

Rack System The system used in mountainous areas whereby the propulsion if effected by the interaction between a cog or pinion on the locomotive and a cogged or rack rail laid between the running rails.

Railcar A self-powered passenger carrying vehicle.

Shay A locomotive design by Michigan logging engineer Ephrain Shay, which was adopted by the Lima Locomotive Works of Ohio.

Shinkansen The Japanese Bullet train

Shunters Small engines used to divert wagons onto a siding, or marshal them into a specific order. Called switchers in the US.

Steam coal Coal which is use as locomotive fuel.

Switchers see Shunters.

Tank engines Locomotives with water tanks on either side of the boiler.

Tender locomotives A steam locomotive with a built-on tender.

TGV Train Grande Vitesse, the French high-speed train.

Wagon ways Usually refers to pre-19th century horse-drawn railways.

Wheel arrangements Steam locomotives are commonly classified according to the White system of notation of wheel arrangement into front wheels, driving wheels and rear wheels. Hence a 4–6–2 has four front wheels, six driving wheels and two rear wheels. The German system of notation only counts the wheels of one side so the above example, in Germany, would be classified 2–3–1.

Zig Zag A method of building a line to achieve height in a mountainous restrictive area.

INDEX

PICTURE ACKNOWLEDGEMENTS

All pictures copyright Milepost 92½ with exception of the following:

Alan Pike 44, 48 bottom, 73 right, 91 top, 154

Andrew Finch 90

Brian Burchell 148, 149 top, 160

Brian Solomon 70 top, 81 right, 85 top, 150, 151, 158 bottom, 179

Bridgeman Art Library 8–9, 10–11, 11 top, 12 top, 14 left, 17, 25 top, 34–35

Canadian Pacific 13 left, 56–57

Christopher Portway 57 top, 62–63

Comstock 4–5

David King Collection 15 top, 48 top, 118 top, 120

David Patterson 172

Glasgow City Council, Mitchell Library 32–33, 51 bottom

Graham Pike 37

Henry Priestley 164–165

Hulton Deutsch 8 bottom

Illustrated London News 34 top, 116, 117, 126, 127 top, 130, 131, 132, 133

Imperial War Museum 118–119, 123, 125 right

International News Service, Tokyo 183

James Harkin 174–175

Jay Williams 68 left

John Scott-Morgan 6, 14–15, 66 top

Marcel Vleugels 64, 72–73

Max Wade-Matthews 115

Melvyn Hopwood 157

Mike Russel 167 right, 175 right

Mike Taplin 162, 168, 169

Musée Français du Chemin du Fer 27

National Railway Museum, York 69

National Tramway Museum, Crich 163

Rev A.W.V. Mace 35 top, 97 bottom, 12 bottom

Steven le Cheminart 124 top

Theo James 176, 181 right

Verkehusmuseum Nurnberg 8 top

W. A. Sharman 65